I0485697

Drawing Awesome Figures For Beginners

Ultimate Guide to Learn Proportions, Poses, Mannequin, Blocking in Figures with Shapes and More

By Kirsten Little

Table of Contents

Disclaimer

While all attempts have been made to verify the information provided in this book, the author does assume any responsibility for errors, omissions, or contrary interpretations of the subject matter contained within. **The information provided in this book is for educational and entertainment purposes only. The reader is responsible for his or her own actions and the author does not accept any responsibilities for any liabilities or damages, real or perceived, resulting from the use of this information.**

The trademarks that are used are without any consent, and the publication of the trademark is without permission or backing by the trademark owner. All trademarks and brands within this book are for clarifying purposes only and are the owned by the owners themselves, not affiliated with this document.

Introduction

There is no right or wrong way to draw the human figure. After the brain absorbs everything you have learned it connects this knowledge in a way that suits it best. Drawing is a unique combination of your own aesthetics, experience and practice. In the following pages you will find some basic techniques that you will need to draw the human figure.

This book is designed as a beginner`s guide to drawing human figures, but it can also serve those who already have some knowledge about drawing figures. If you`re some sort of drawing guru, and most of us aren`t, than this book is not for you.

The book that is before you represents extensive research on how to draw the human figure. In this book, in addition to advice on how to choose the right paper and pens for drawing, you will also find instructions, supported by pictures, on following subjects:

- Short history of proportions
- Drawing basic shapes and human figures
- Male and female figures
- Proportions

- How to draw a mannequin

- Anatomy or how to add muscles

- Poses (three step-by-step poses)

- Blocking in the figure with shapes

- Links for sites about art of drawing

Drawing is not for talented people only, it`s primarily for those who like to draw and are willing to practice it.

Chapter 1 - Paper, Pencils, and other Implements

Paper for Drawing

Although for drawing you can use almost any paper, you need to know some basic features of drawing paper because different mediums such as graphite pencil, colored pencils, watercolor, ink, and so on require different types of paper to achieve maximum effect. The high-quality paper itself should be labeled indicating all of its features, and when in the form of block-paper often has a label that indicates which techniques are suitable.

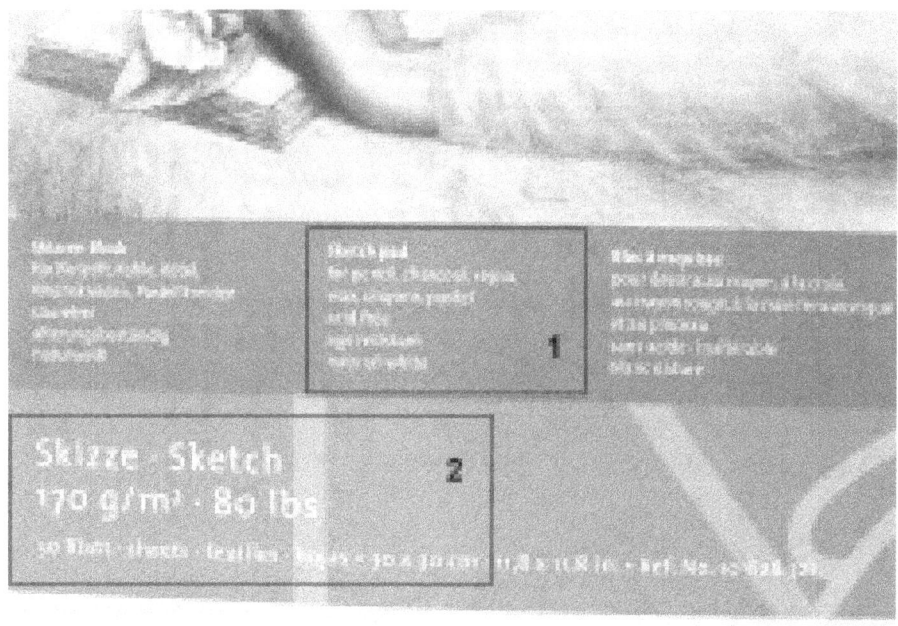

The picture above is block drawing paper on which I labeled the mark of quality and the pictures below show marks followed by a description of these qualities.

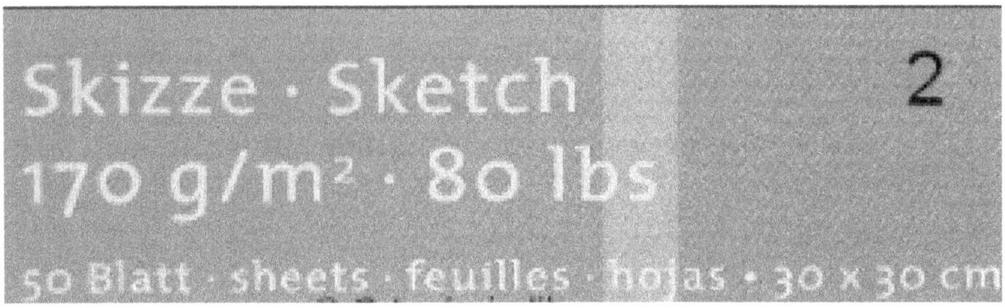

Skizze · Sketch 2
170 g/m² · 80 lbs
50 Blatt · sheets · feuilles · hojas · 30 x 30 cm

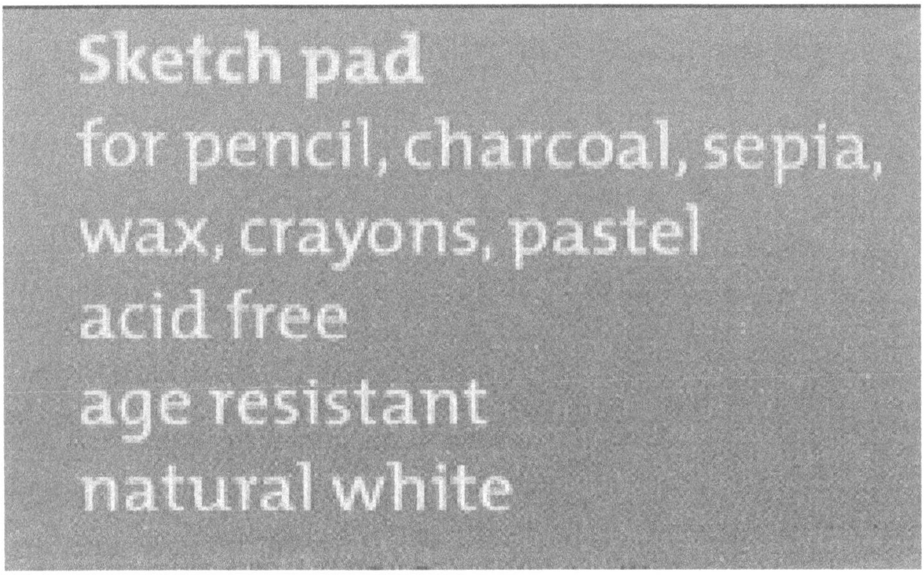

Sketch pad
for pencil, charcoal, sepia,
wax, crayons, pastel
acid free
age resistant
natural white

Weight and Thickness of the Paper

Paper thickness is measured in grams per square meter and is produced in the range of 80g/m² for drawing, up to more than 300g/m² which is used for the so-called "aqueous techniques" such as watercolor.

The block papers are produced in sizes from A6 to A1 (you can see standard sizes below). They usually have at least one hard cover what makes drawing easier.

A0 - 841mm x 1189mm

A1 - 594mm x 841mm

A2 - 420mm x 594mm

A3 - 297mm x 420mm

A4 - 210mm x 297mm

A5 - 148mm x 210mm

A6 - 105mm x 148mm

Surface Roughness

Roughness is one of the most important characteristics of paper because it depends on how much graphite or other media will adhere to the paper. Rough paper is labeled as "cold press" and can be divided into three levels of roughness; slightly roughened, medium roughened, and extremely roughened surface. The last one is used for drawing with soft media such as charcoal, chalk or pastel.

Durability

Labels on paper such as "Acid-free", "Age-resistant" or "Archival quality" suggests that it is a high-quality paper that will not fall apart and will not become yellow over time.

The Color of the Paper

Drawing paper is manufactured in a large range of colors. For drawing with a pencil, is mainly used the so-called "natural white", which unlike copier paper, has a very mild gray or yellow tint, depending on from what kind of raw material is made.

Regardless of whether you buy paper for drawing in the form of a block or a piece always look for a label on it that indicate the characteristics of the paper.

Choosing the Right Paper

For exercise, you can use any paper, starting from ordinary notebooks with or without lines, copier paper, or school sketchpad in all sizes. The ideal paper for working with pencils is in the range from $110g/m^2$ to $180g/m^2$ with a slightly roughened or medium roughened surface.

The slicker paper looks quite nice and feels pleasant to the touch but isn`t good for drawing because the graphite is not able hold on to it tightly and pencil can deviate on its smooth surface making it impossible to draw.

If you love doing photo-realistic drawings then get a thicker, medium roughened paper as this way of drawing is seeking for permanent corrections with an eraser. If the paper is thin or rough it can be damaged.

It is desirable for you to obtain a pair of blocks with a spiral for sketching. Try to make sure that the quality is excellent and that they have at least one cover of hard cardboard which makes them good for transport and drawing on the spot. The papers are easily removed from a spiral so that you can continue with the drawing on the table or if the drawing is finished you can shelter or frame your work.

Make sure you get one block of A5 format (15x21cm) with a hard cover as it is perfect for carrying and sketching.

Pencils

The main characteristic of all pencils is the hardness of graphite. The graphite heart is a mixture of graphite and clay, and depending on the amount of clay the pencil leaves a lighter or darker trail. The ratio of clay and graphite divides pencils into hard, which are marked "H" and leave lighter tracks, medium with the tags "F" and "HB", and soft with the tag "B" which have more graffiti inside and leave a darker track. The number next to the letter indicates the degree of hardness with 9H being the hardest and 9B as the softest.

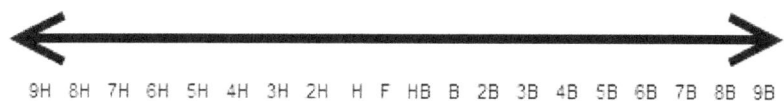

9H 8H 7H 6H 5H 4H 3H 2H H F HB B 2B 3B 4B 5B 6B 7B 8B 9B

For sketching and drawing details, so called "wooden pens" (No.1) are mainly used and can be found in all levels of hardness. For filling large areas and drawing on large paper, graphite coated with plastic wrap (No.2) and graphite rod (No.3) are used. Be careful with these pieces of graphite because they are comparatively easy to break.

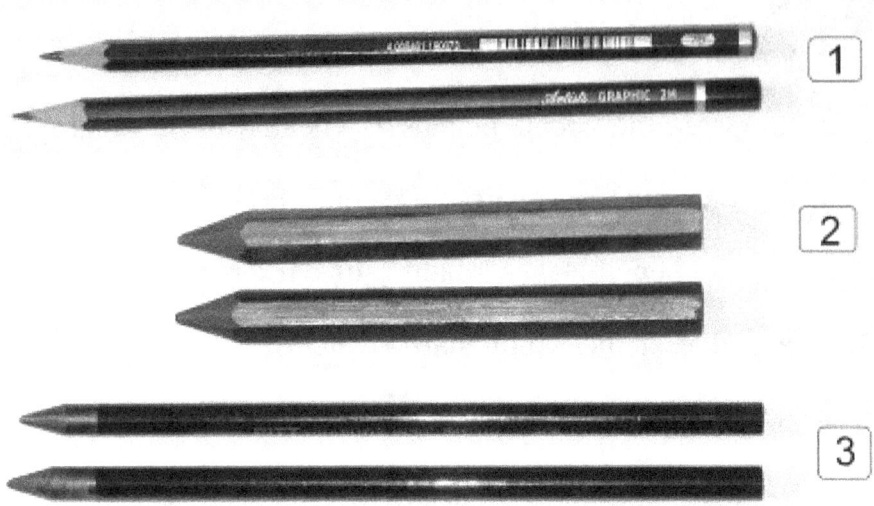

Technical pens (No.4) are used for drawing fine details and are practical because they do not need constant sharpening. Pencils with a charcoal heart (No.5) leave an intense black track and are used as the medium itself or in combination with other techniques.

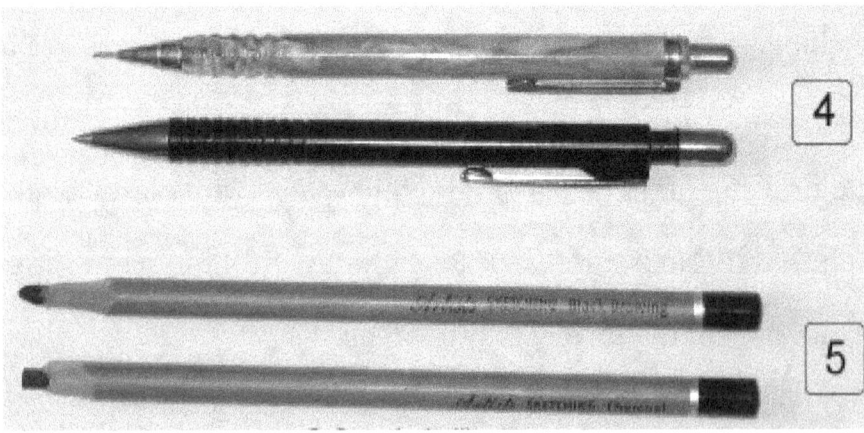

Purchasing Pens

Since the most important part of drawing is the pencil, never try save on this implement. Believe me; you do not want to see scratches and unwanted dark lines on your paper that cheap pens can leave. High-quality pens can be identified by marks such are "Artist quality" or "Fine Art" or another identifiers that indicates the quality. At the beginning it will be quite sufficient for you to have three quality pencils, hardness 4H, HB, and 4B.

Mannequin doll

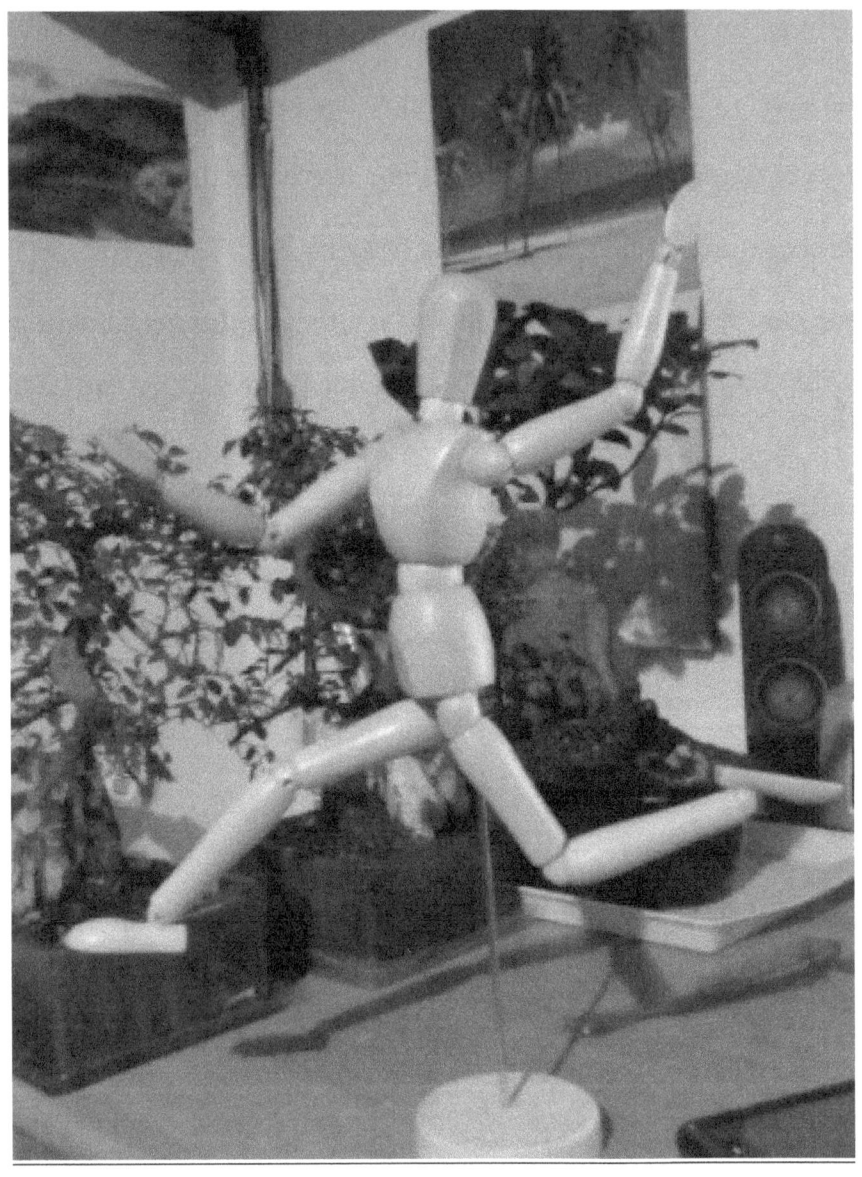

If your subject of interest is the human figure, it would be good for you to have a painter's doll, or "mannequin". Training on the mannequin is the best way to learn the proportions of the human body in almost all the positions that it can take. You can buy a mannequin in specialized shops which sell artists' materials.

Warming up

All great athletes warm up before a match. As an artist you also need to warm up before drawing. To relax your hands and have more success in drawing takes a little practice. Pictured below are two exercises to relax your hands and warm up before drawing. Exercise one is on the first picture. You should do it fast and in one stroke, first clockwise and then counterclockwise. On the second picture is the exercise called "Do a pose as fast as you can". It`s just an exercise, it doesn`t mean you`re a bed drawer.

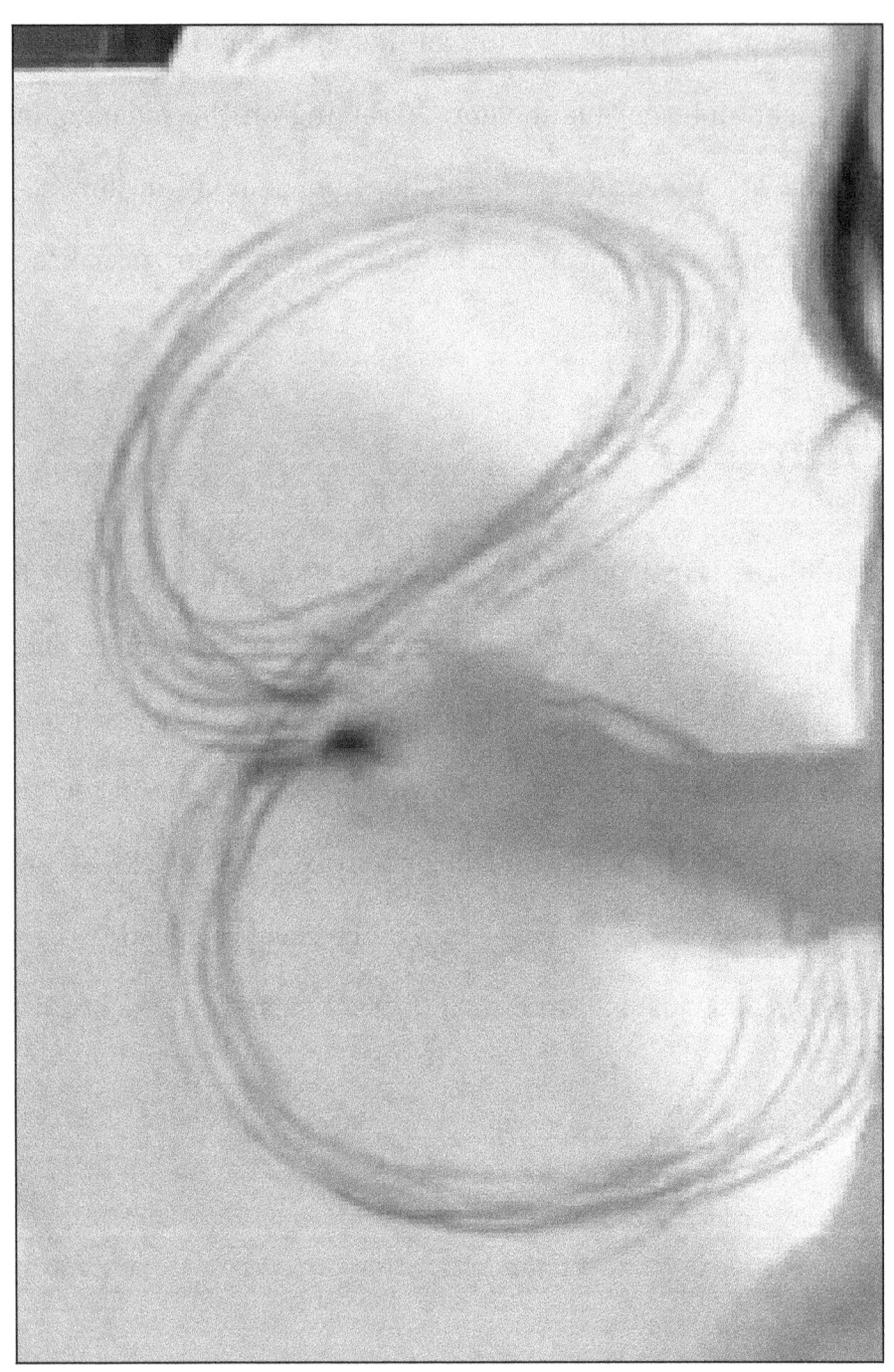

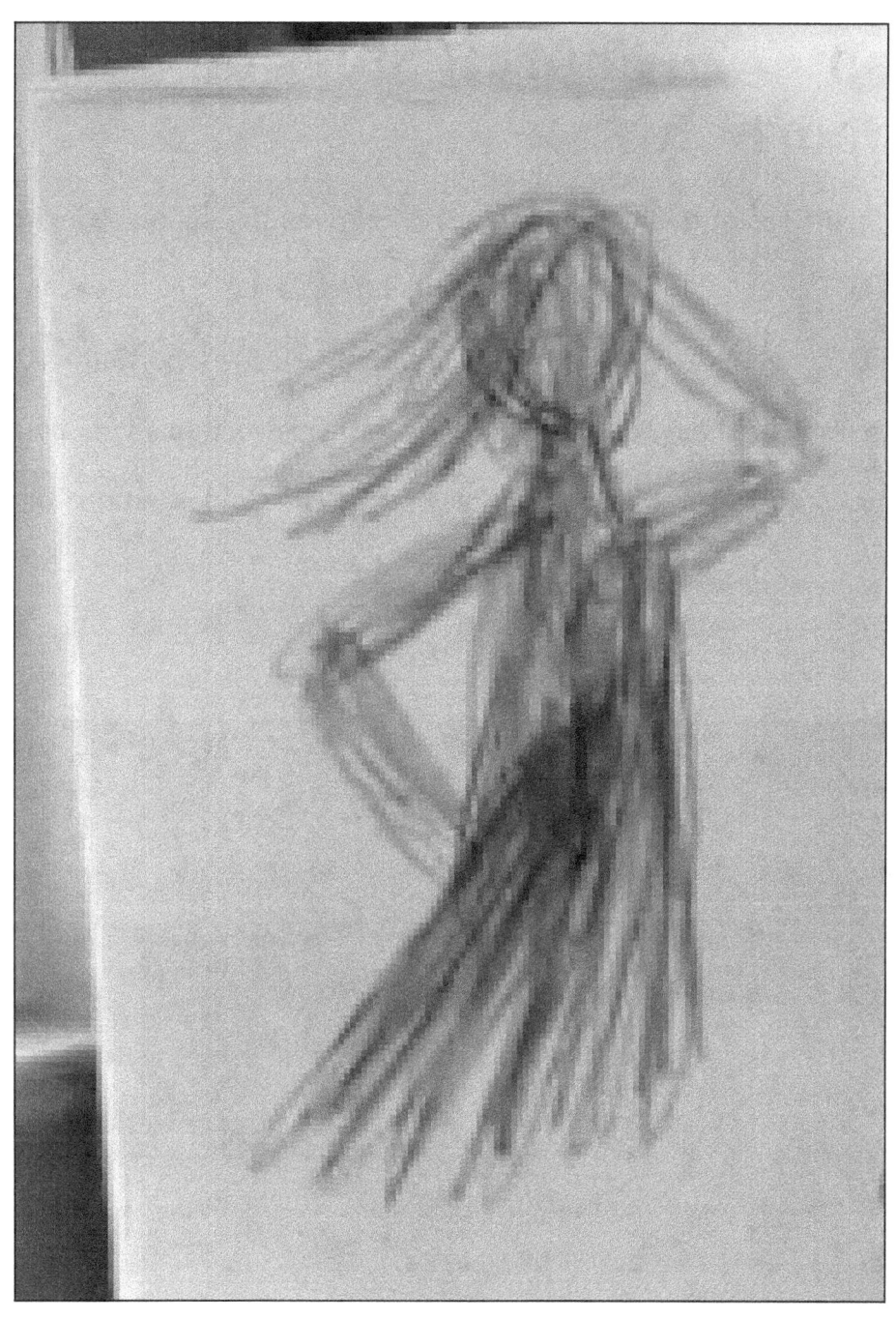

Picture source: YouTube-Heather Le Bas

Chapter 2 - Short History of Proportion

The proportions of the human body have been studied by many artists and scientists throughout history. In ancient Greece and Egypt, it was believed that the human body followed a principle of perfect proportion called the "golden ratio", which was also used in the construction of monumental buildings such as pyramids or the Parthenon. The Golden ratio is the ratio between two line segments A and B where $\frac{A}{B} = \frac{A+B}{A}$.

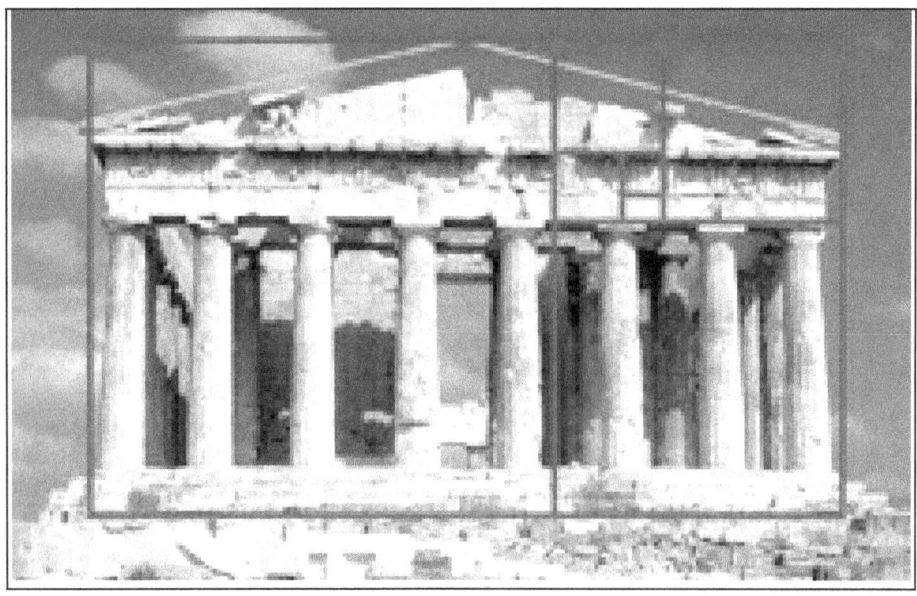

Modern scientists have sought to prove that this principle occurs spontaneously in nature as well as that it can be found in of all periods of art, even when artists had not yet discovered the appropriate mathematical rules.

When talking about the unity of the human body as a synonym for the symmetry of the visual field, the art of classical Greece is the clear place to begin. In the 4th century BC the sculptor Polycleitus of Argos, credited as one of creators of the classic Greek style of art, freed what we think of as Greek beauty from the ether. He created a style of sculpture, known as the "Canon", which glorified the athletic male body and relied upon counterbalance of body parts.

After Polycleitus fixed units were no longer used, rather proportions were considered according to the ratio of one body part to another. This organic concept won out over coldness the Egyptian style while adapting itself to a viewer.

Art in the Middle Ages was committed to religion subjects was dedicated to God. The rise of Humanism during the Renaissance overcame this attitude towards religion and placed man at the forefront of research.

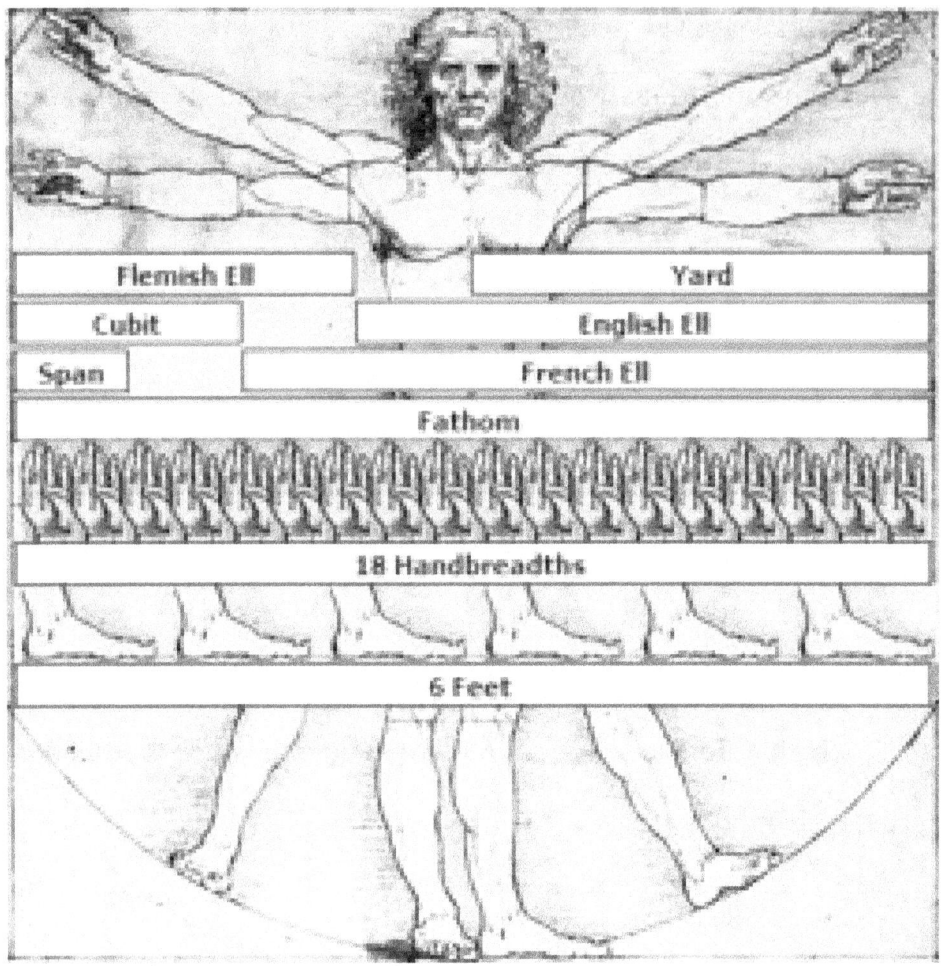

Leonardo da Vinci and Albrecht Dürer are artists who re-established the Greek concept of the relationship of ideal measures, which remains unsurpassed even today. Da Vinci's drawing of the Vitruvian man is a prime example of the use of these measures.

This drawing represents man's connection with both the world around him by depicting a human body filling the space of both a circle, which represented the spiritual world, and the square, which represented the natural world. Da Vinci's proportions are based on old idealized measures of human body parts located in the following proportions: height = 8 heads, palm = 4 fingers, foot = 4 palms, arm span = height, face = 1/10 height; shoulder width = 1/4 height.

The Middle Ages exuded the worship God. Dürer insisted on a religious conception of reality in which the pure and simple truth about things is found within their mathematical relations. That attitude has a broader reflection on his work.

In Dürer's conception, the body proportions, just like the mathematical order found in nature, are based on rigorous mathematical patterns. His famous painting Melancholia 1 combines the melancholic character of inspiration with geometric elements and mathematical order which Dürer held so highly. Dürer, arguably the most famous artist of the German Renaissance, was not just limited to painting and drawing. He also wrote a work on geometry, perspective, proportion and the design of fortifications.

Chapter 3 - Drawing Basic Shapes and Human Figures

Practicing Basic Shapes

All that is found in nature is composed of geometric shapes. If you want to learn how to draw anything, even the human figure, you first have to master drawing these basic geometric shapes. Although you might think that there is nothing easier than this, you should still practice as much as possible.

The more you practice drawing basic shapes the more successful you will be in drawing figures. These are the basics of drawing: everything you want to draw can be made by using squares, triangles, circles, ellipses, cones, and cylinders. These geometric shapes will help you start building the figure or whatever you wish to draw.

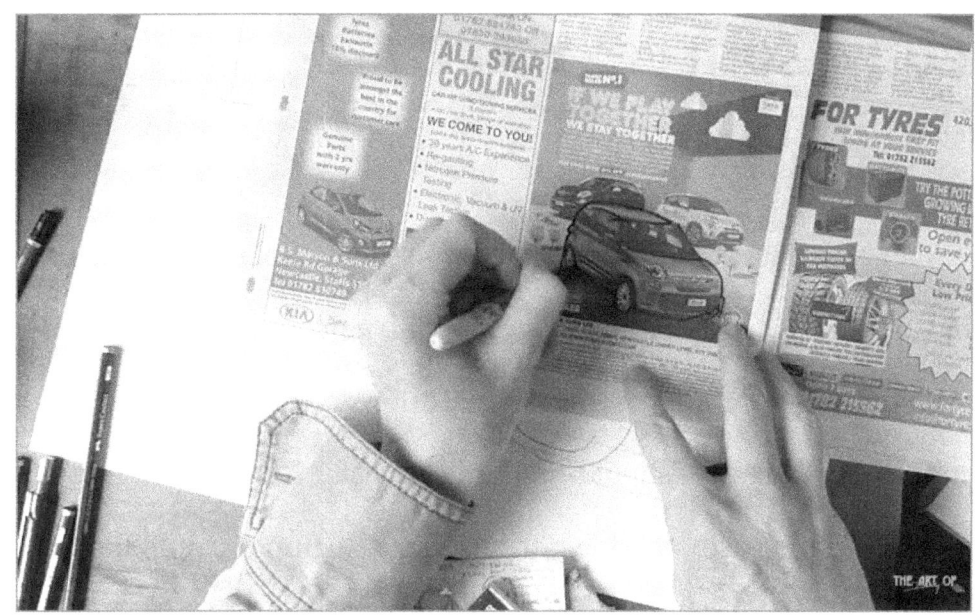

Don`t be afraid to use a ruler or anything that has a circle or any other shape to help you learn how to draw geometric shapes free hand. You can use a penny, an duct tape roll, a book, and so on.

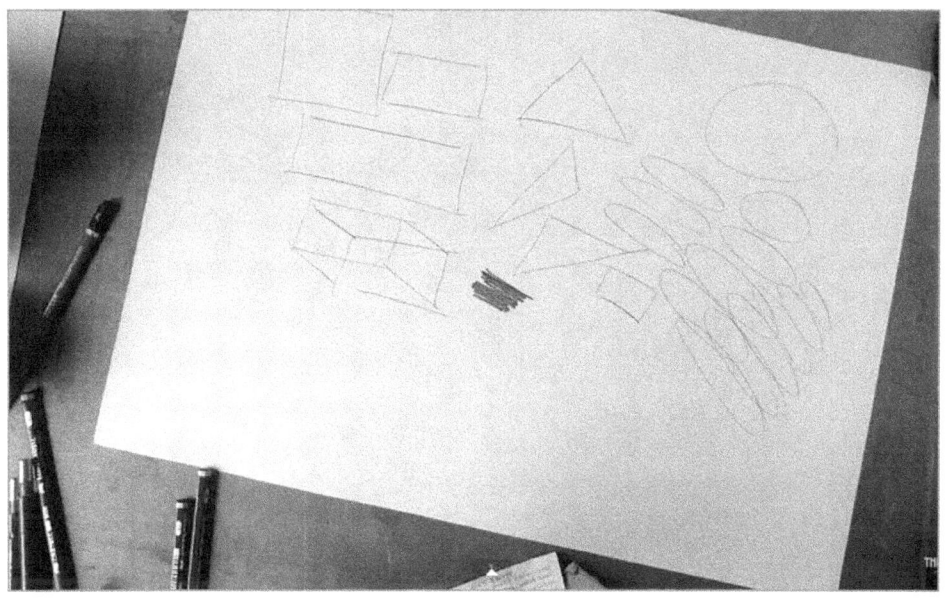

Picture source: YouTube-theartofbilly

You can also practice drawing shapes on newspapers. Just draw lines around objects you see pictured. This will help your hand get used to drawing the different shapes that make up every day things. If you`re a beginner at drawing, you should first draw objects like this before you move on to figures. It is easily the biggest mistake a beginner can make to try to start drawing without first learning these fundamentals.

Basic Male and Female Figures

We'll start with drawing a male figure. First draw a regular circle for the head, then curved line which will represent the backbone. Below draw a box for the head and shoulders. As we draw the male figure, this part will be bigger than the rectangle that will represent pelvis.

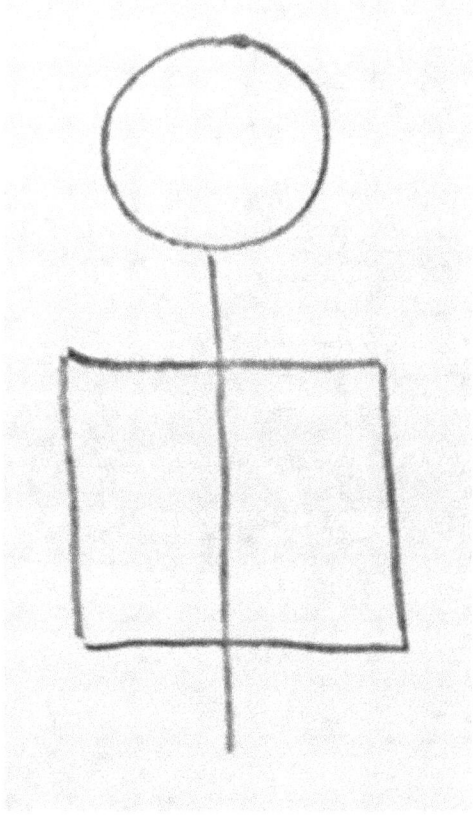

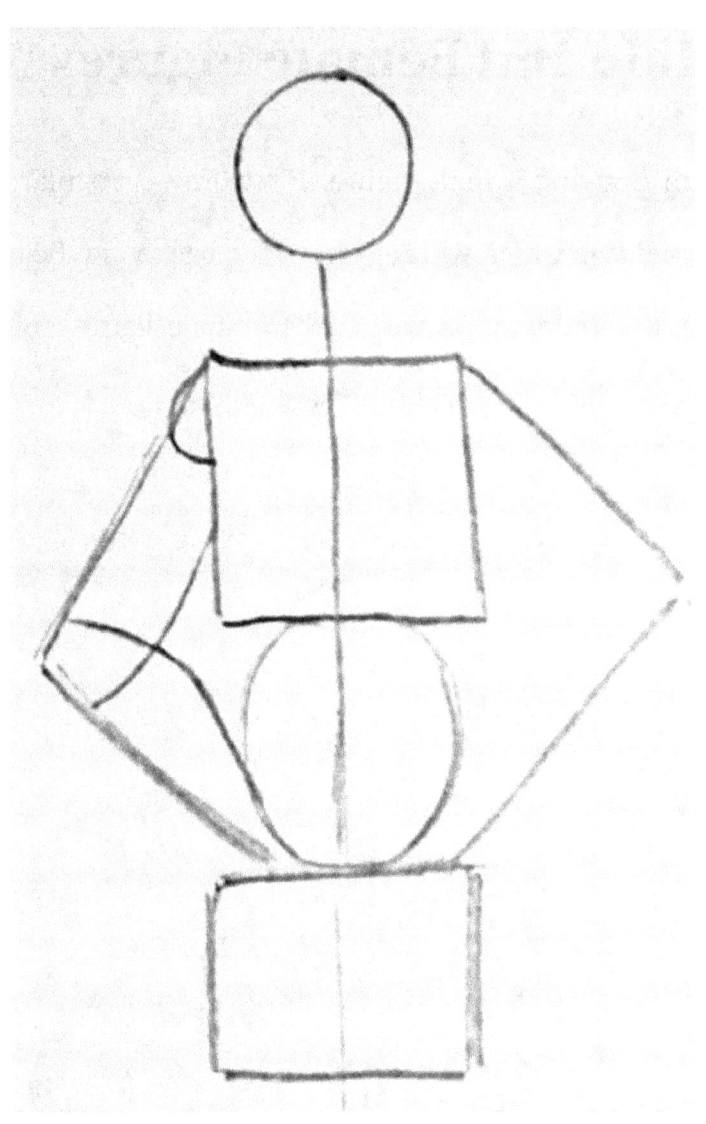

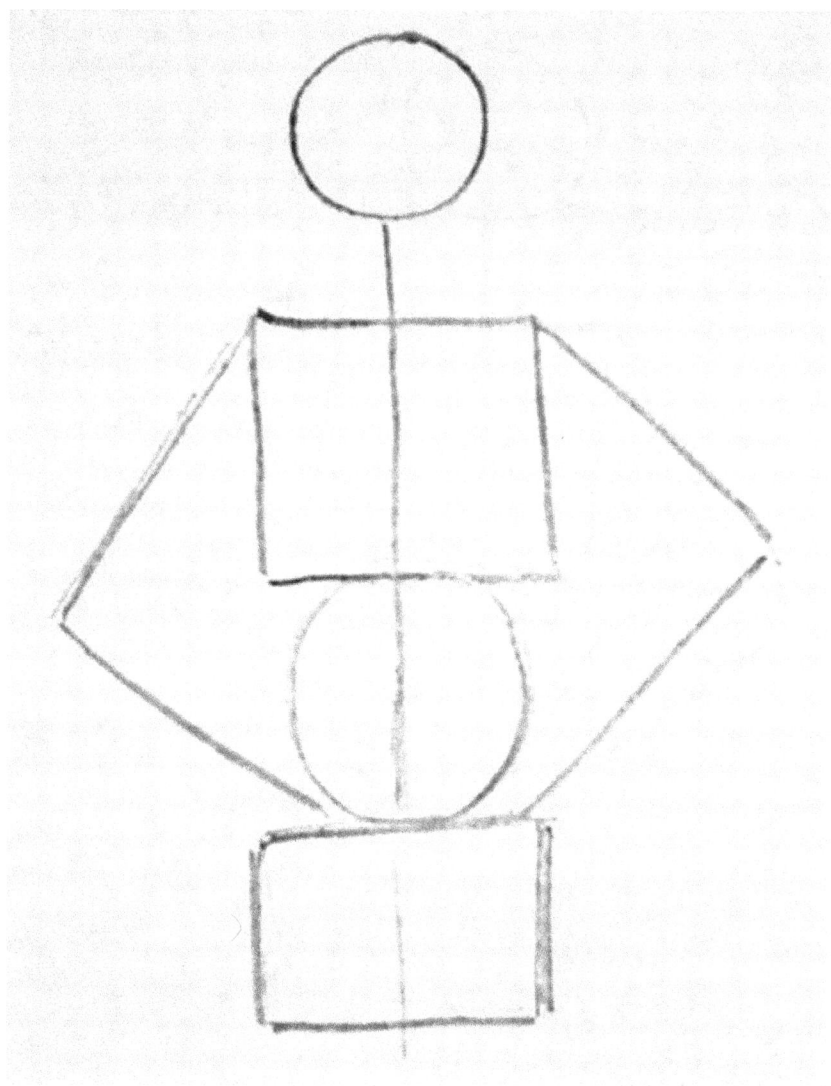

We continue by drawing arms. As this will be male figure the arms will be more masculine.

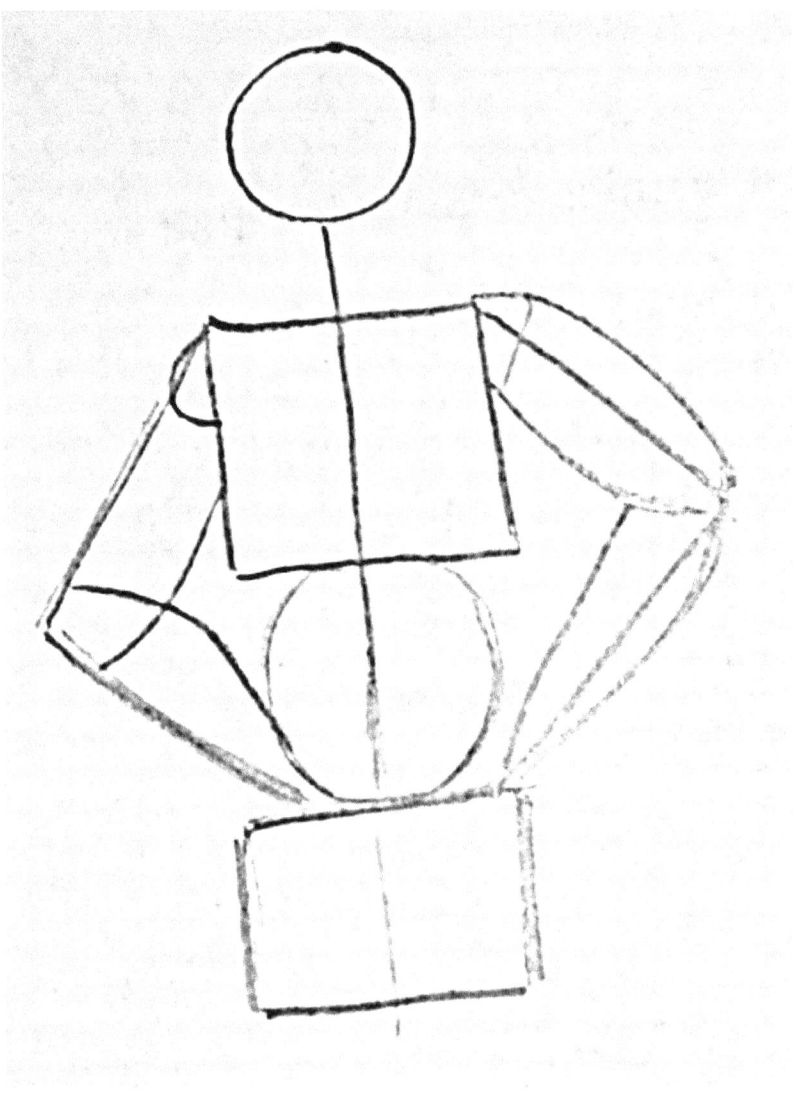

Now, we will draw legs and the rest of the basic male figure.

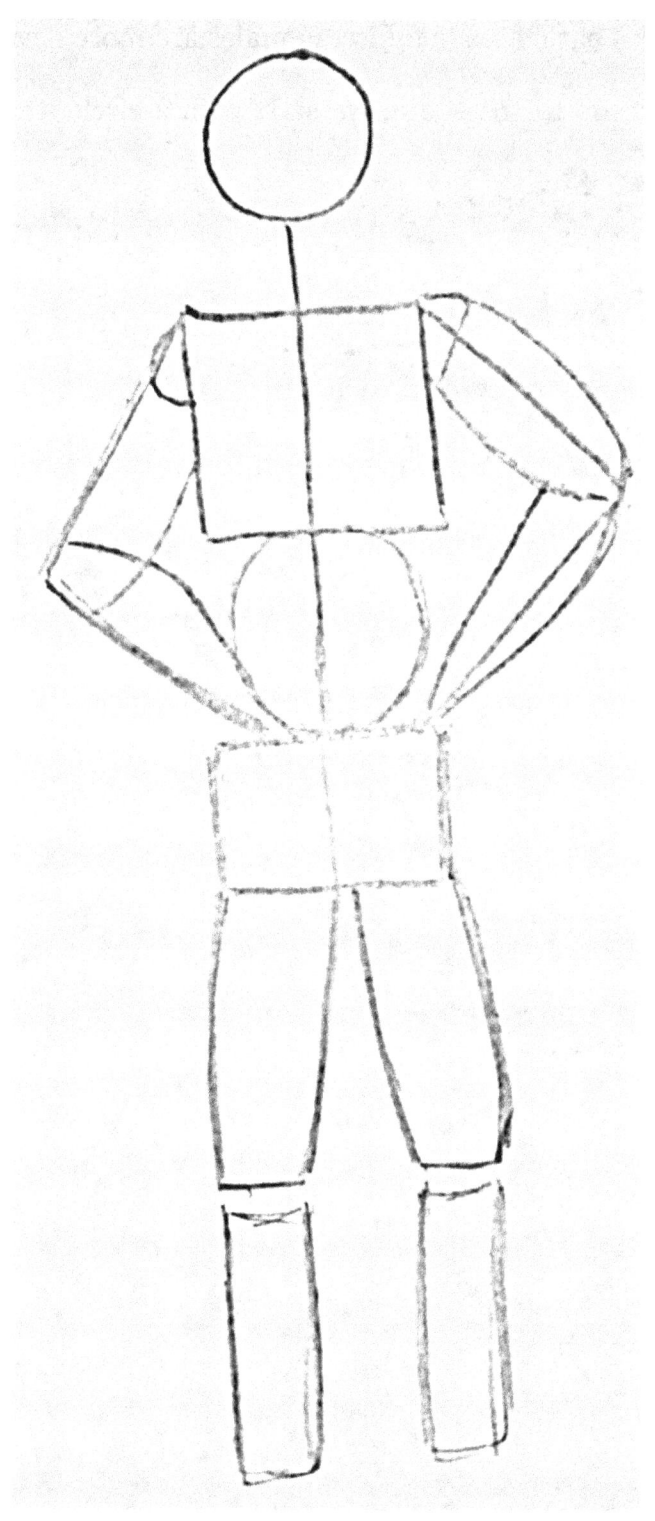

Next, let`s draw a basic female figure. Females are more developed in pelvis area than in the top torso. Again, we start with a circle, the spine is more curved.

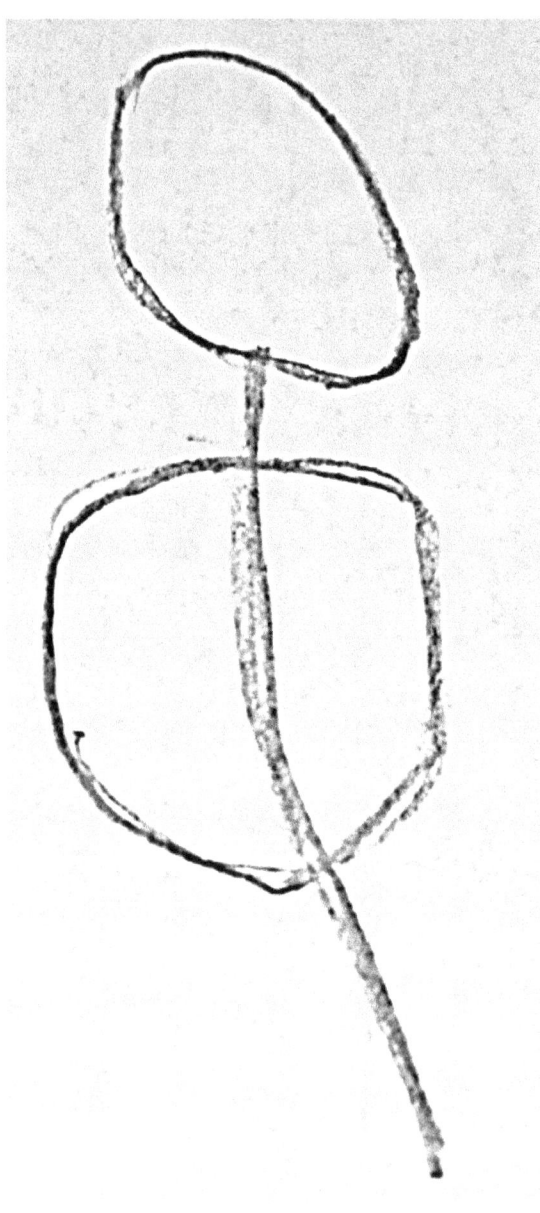

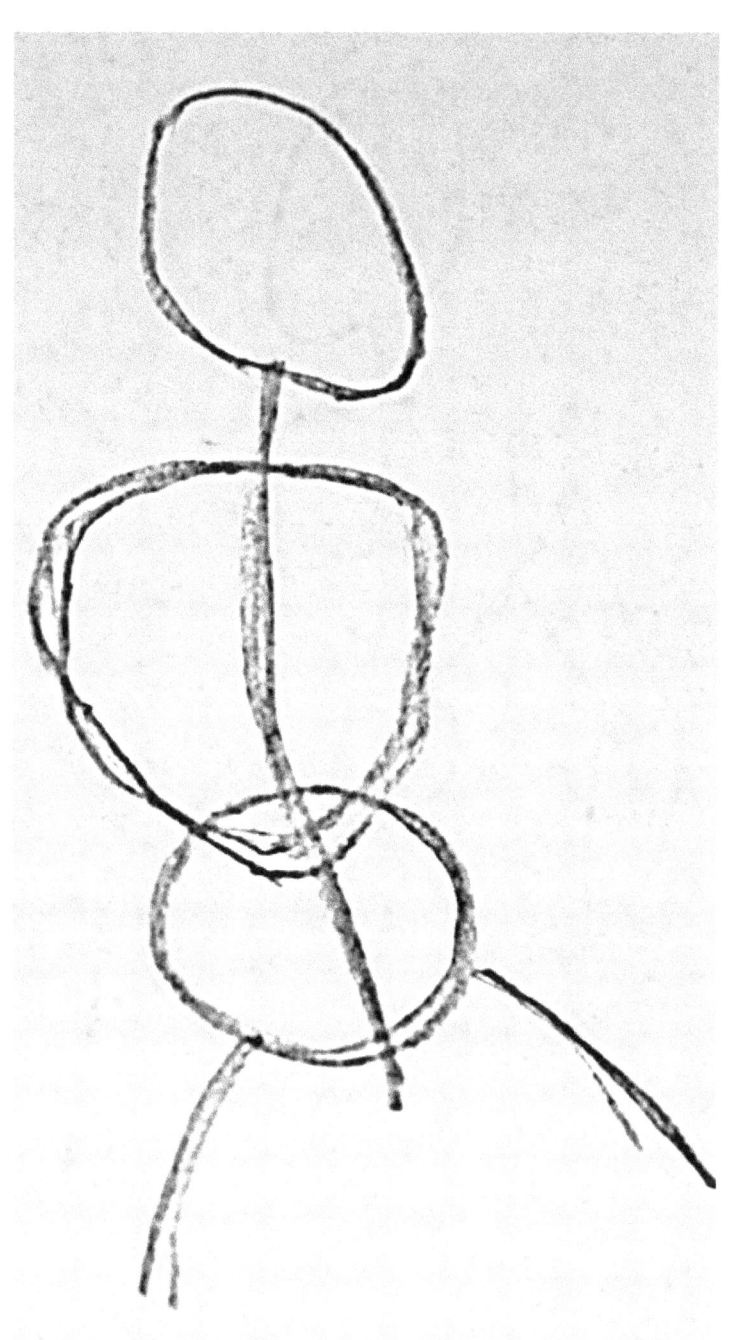

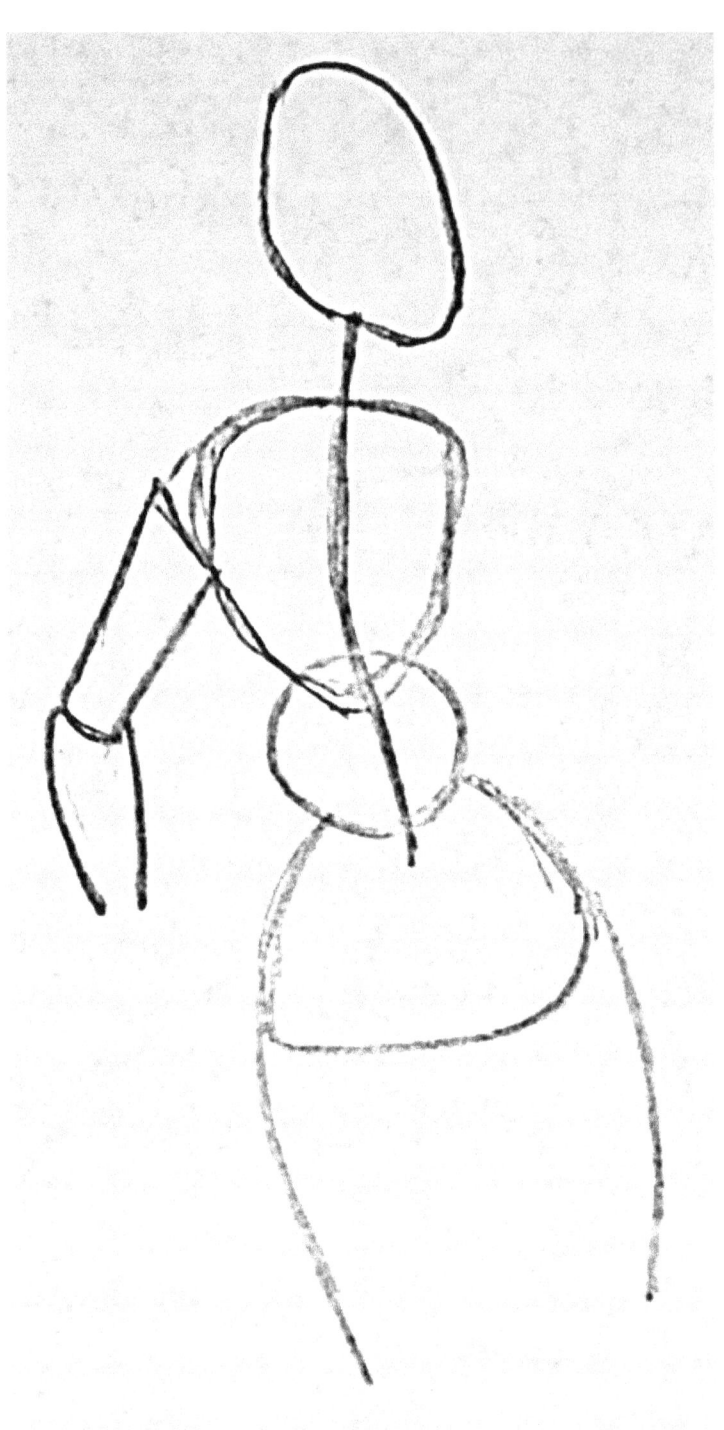

Now, we will draw a pelvis that is similar to a top torso, but upside down, arms and legs. Just follow pictures from left to right.

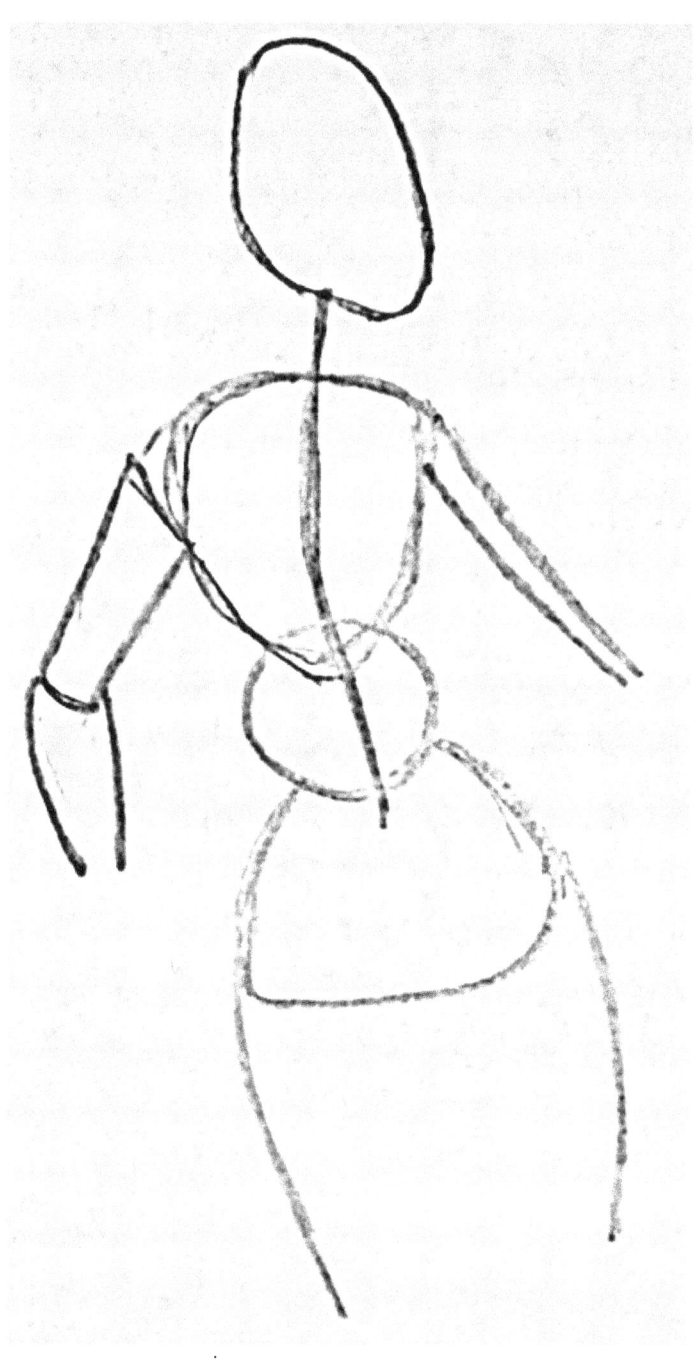

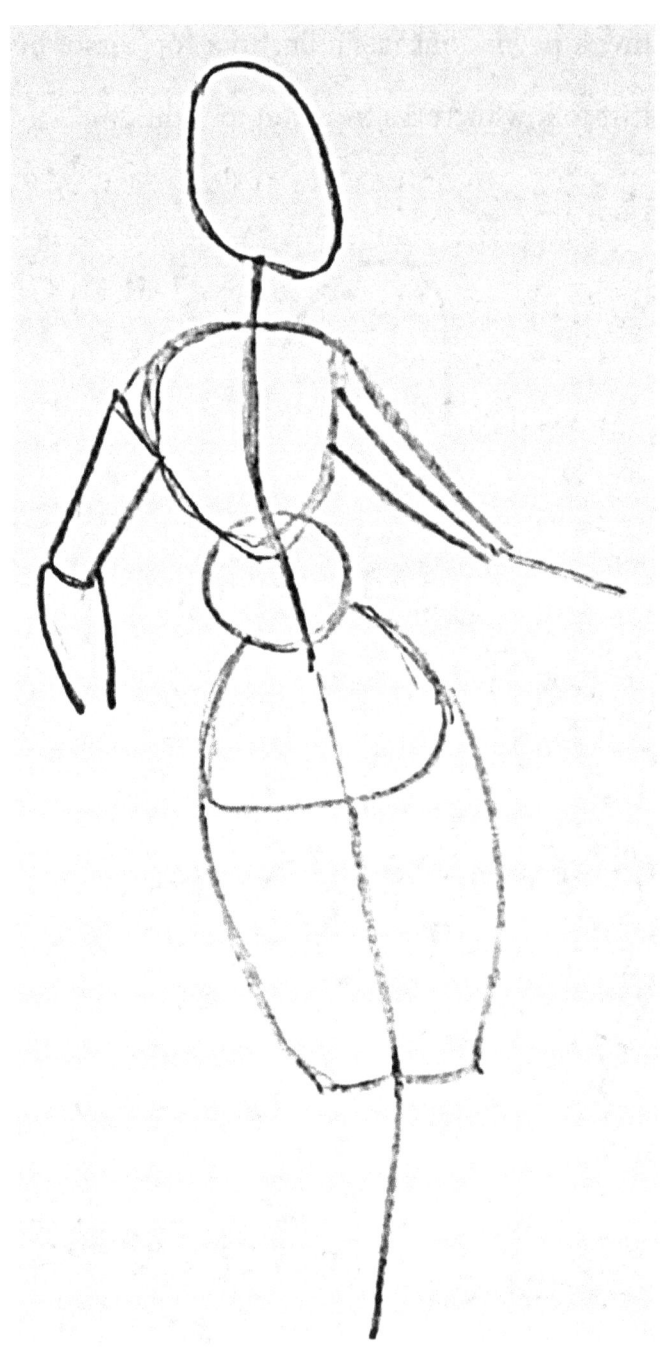

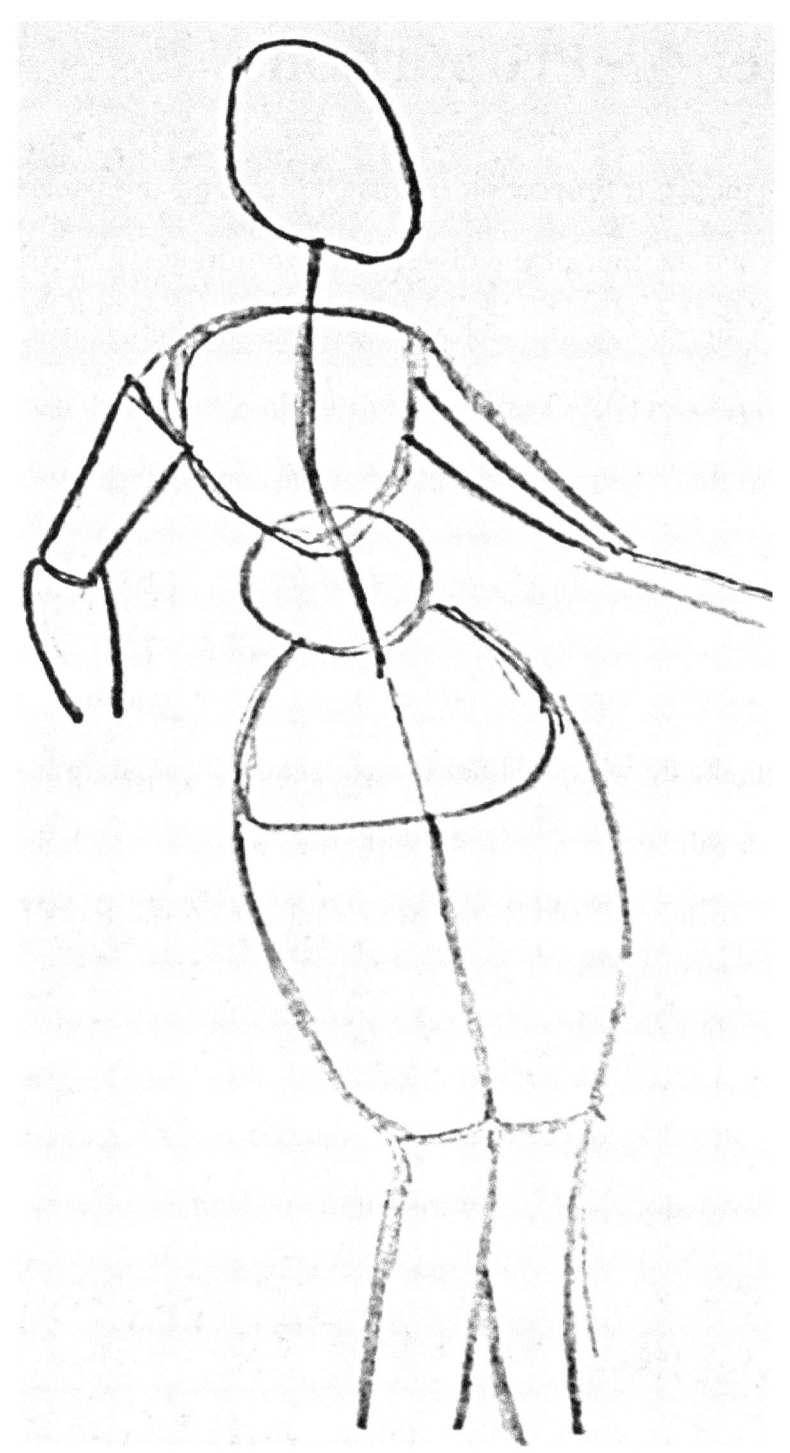

Chapter 4 – Proportions

In drawing, the word proportion means the scale on the paper of the real relations to one another of the objects that you draw. The proportion is a relation of dimensions of an object, regardless of whether it is a house, a figure of a man, etc. The easiest way to explain the relationship between length and width or height is by looking at the simple objects with the right edges.

On the left in the picture below is the house with an imaginary height of 12 meters. To make drawing this house easier, we will separate it into simple shapes which will be easier to work with, the rectangle which makes up the bottom two stories and the tringle which makes up the top story and the roof.

These will also be given imaginary dimensions of 7 and 5 meters respectively. To draw a true representation of this house, you have to replicate that aspect ratio of these two dimensions, that is to say 7:5. Otherwise, your house will not look like the house in the picture.

If the height of your drawing is approximately 24cm, then to draw this house with accurate proportions the other two dimensions should be 14cm and 10cm which will maintain the ration we determined from the original, that is 7:5 = 14:10

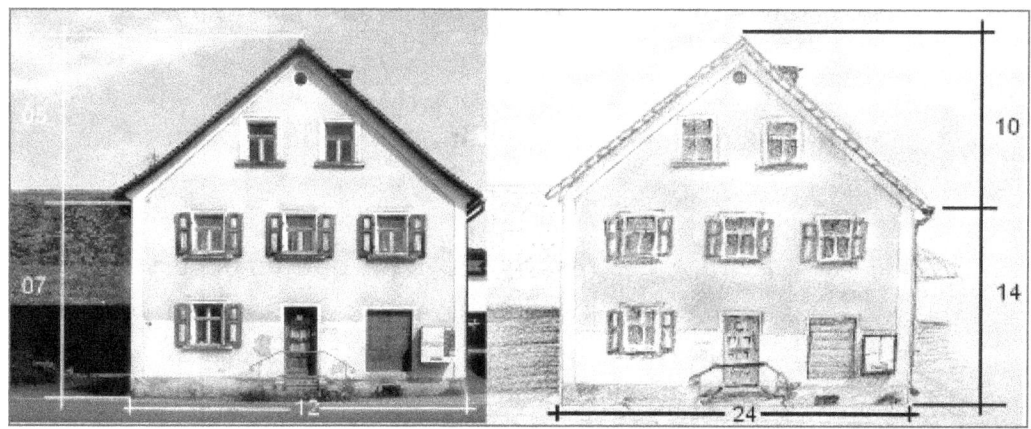

The whole story about human proportion is also reduced to an imaginary ideal human figure in order to become acquainted with drawing human proportions. After you perfect such proportions it is easier to draw a real person who does not comply with this ideal.

When we talk about the body, the head is taken as the basic unit of measurement or one "part", and, therefore, the human figure is divided into seven and a half parts or eighths. Here are a few more ideal rules for drawing a human figure:

- Eyes are placed on the horizontal axis of the head.

- The torso starts with the neck and ends with the navel at the bottom of the third part.

- The torso should be drawn with a width of two parts.

- The pelvis starts at the bottom of the third part and ends at the bottom of the fourth, which makes it one part long.

- The thighs begin at the bottom of part four and taper as the go down nearly two parts, ending above the bottom of the sixth part.

- The knees are also slightly above the bottom of part six.

- The lower leg starts at the bottom of the knee at the end of part six and ends at the bottom of part seven.

- The ankle and foot make up the eighth and final part.

- Extended arm are three and a half parts long, starting from the shoulder and extending to the fingertips on the hands.

- An outstretched hand comprises less than one full part

These are just general instructions and, of course, you do not need a ruler to measure, but if you wish, use a ruler.

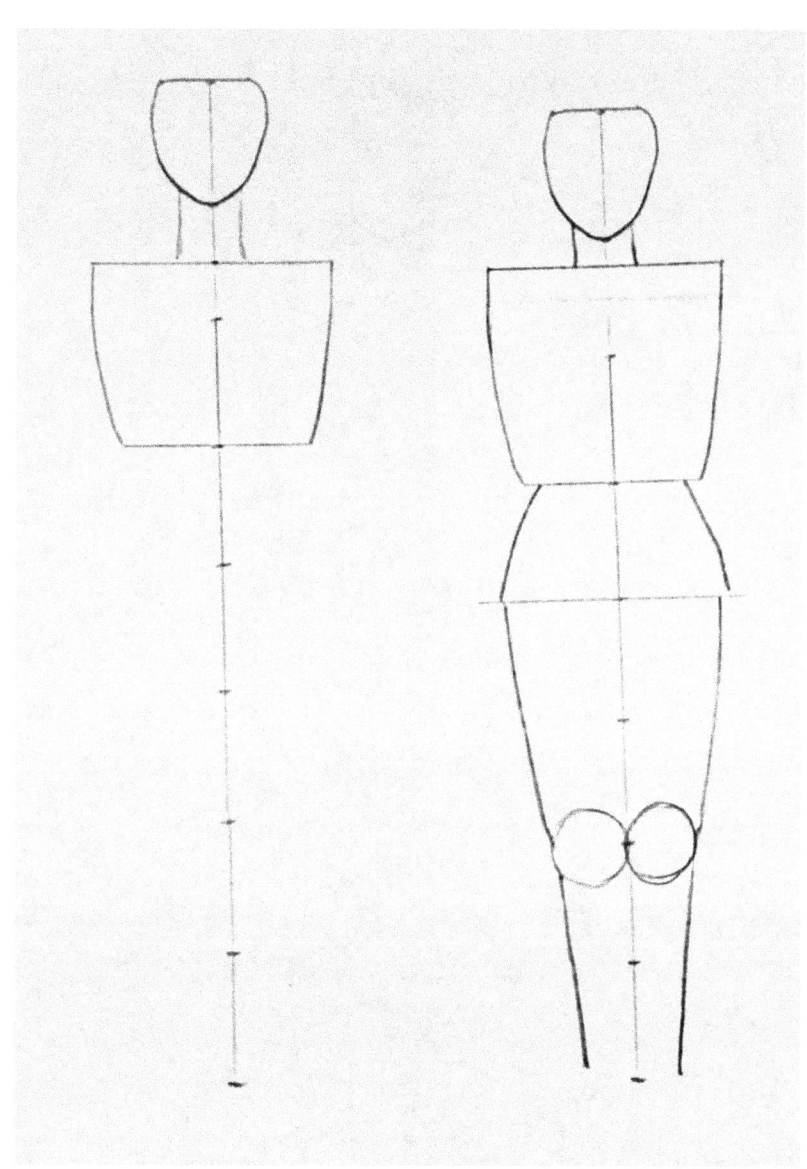

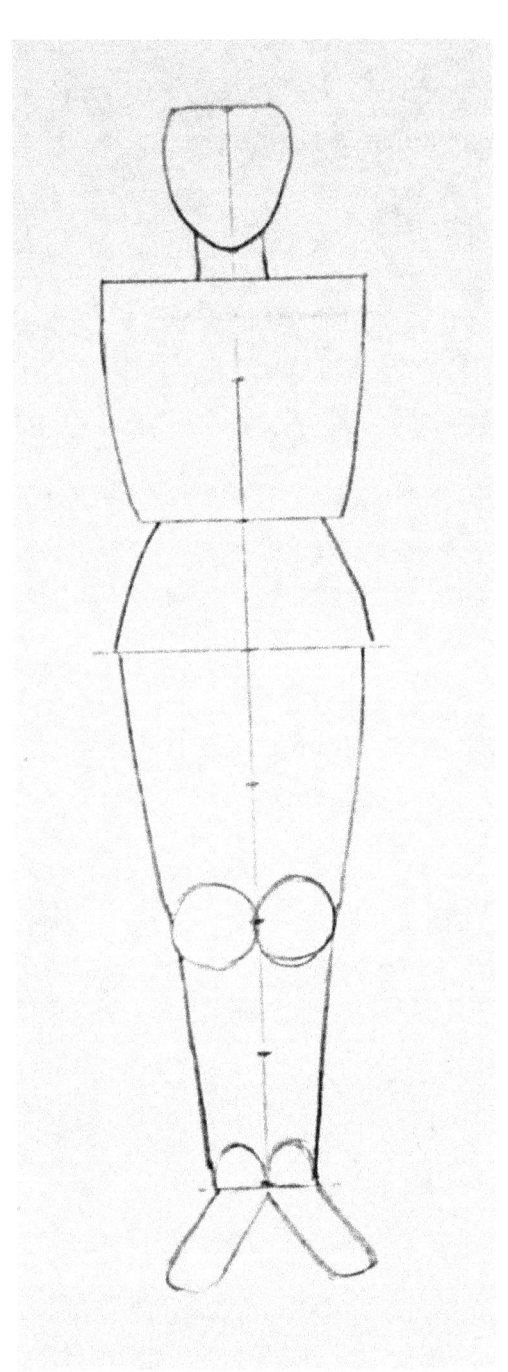

Height of a human figure counts eight heads, so we will first draw a vertical line and divide it into eight equal sections. One section is equal to one head, so first draw a circle in the top section of the line. The neck is one quarter of the head. The shoulders are twice as wide as the head is long. The chest takes two parts and the pelvis takes one part. The legs take up four parts; the two parts beginning at the hips are is joined with the two parts ending at the ankles by the knees.

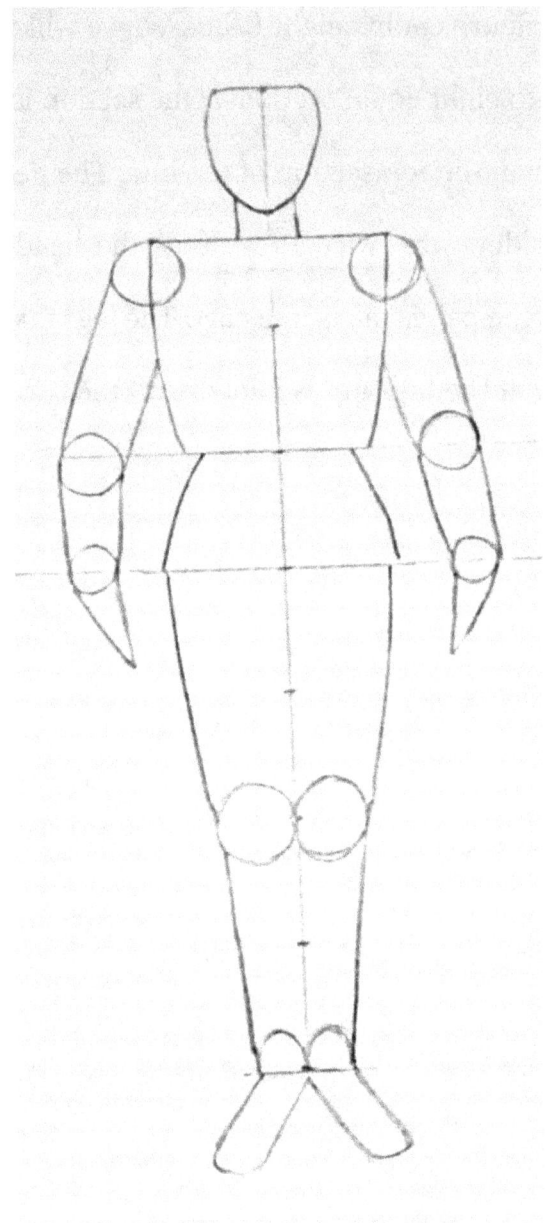

The leg below the knee is not quite a full two parts long, so be sure to leave space for feet at the bottom of the eighth part. Now, we will start drawing arms.

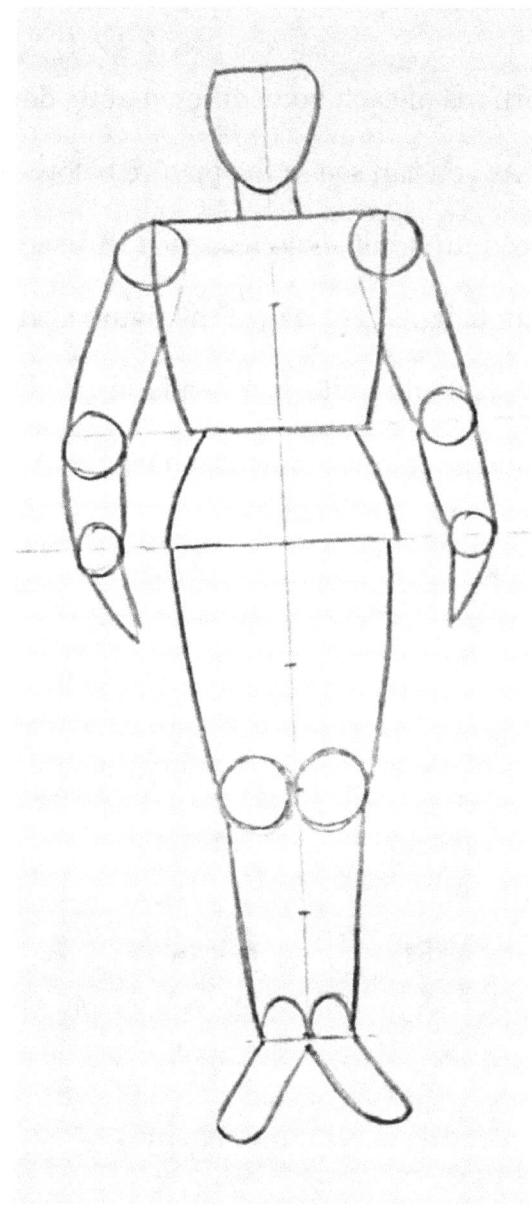

Joints are represented with circles. The upper part of the arm begins at the shoulder and stops at the elbow and the forearm begins at the elbow and ends at the wrist. Each of these joints should be indicated with a circle. The last picture shows the complete figure using these idealized proportions.

Lastly, the proportions of each body differ slightly depending on the age and sex of the figure. As you can see in the picture below, there are differences in proportion between an adult male (8 heads in height) and adult female (7 and a half heads in height). The age of the figure also effects the proportions of the body; a 12 year-old child is 7 heads in height, 6 year-old child is 6 heads in height, and an infant is 4 heads in height

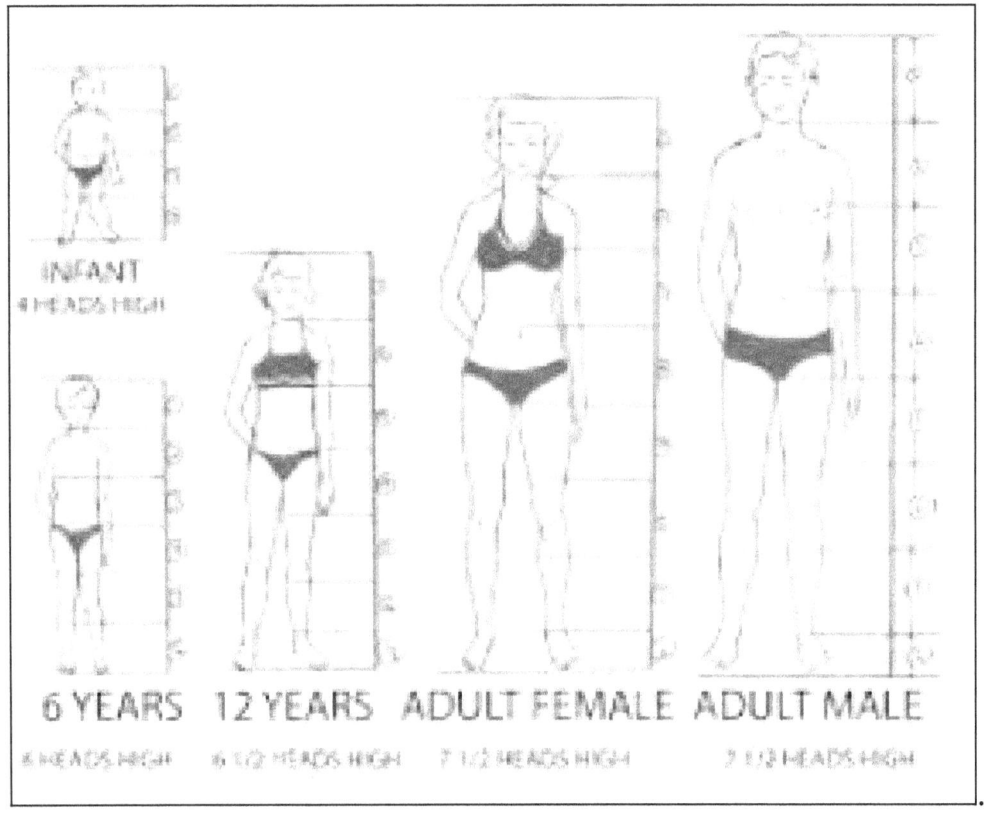

Human head proportions

Portrait of a man's head drawn facing forward is also called the Anfas. This word is of French origin (en face) and free translation would be "in the face".

Just like everything else, when you draw a portrait, you can use the dimension of a part of the face as a unit of measure that will determine all other measurements. To draw portraits of man's face artists have discovered that the ideal unit is the length of the eye. With an eye length, you can exactly determine all other features of the face. In the following text, for simplification rather than the term "length of the eye," I`ll use the term "measure", and you should know that it means the length equal to one eye.

Please bear in mind that this scheme is only a general guide to the proportions and scale of the face and that it varies from head to head. Each person is a little different and each head is different. The differences, however, are often so small that you have to be very careful while drawing that the figure resembled the original.

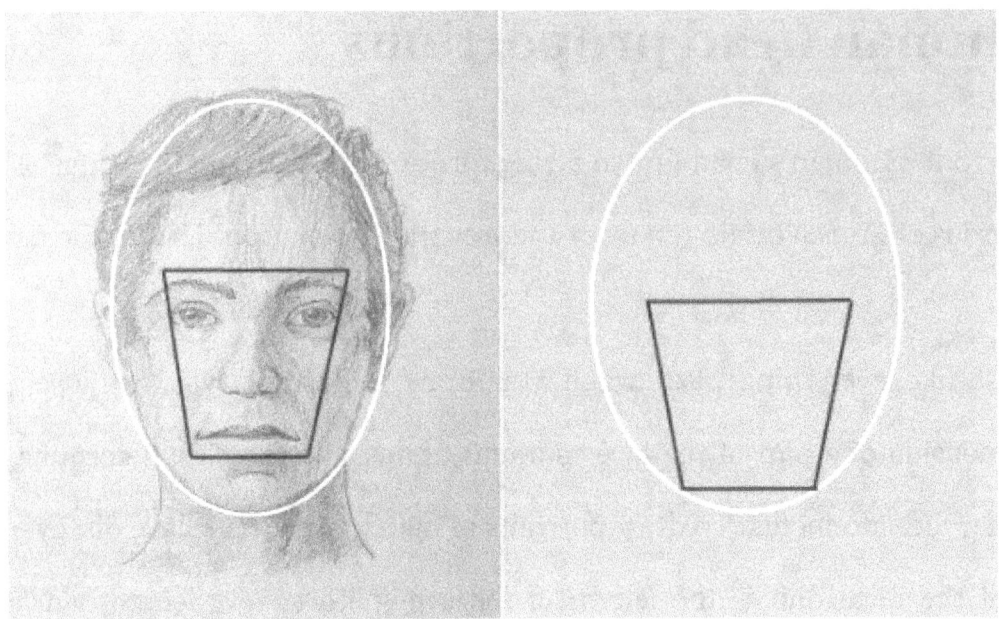

Because of the importance of information that we get from other people through their facial expressions, primarily from the eyes, almost everyone who first draws portraits has a tendency to exaggerate the facial characteristics. So usually, when you first draw a freehand portrait, the eyes, mouth, and nose dominate the face.

This is not, in reality, how a face is composed. On the contrary, as you can see in the picture above, facial characteristics; that is eyes, eyebrows, noses, and mouth, occupy about 1/3 of the entire surface of the head.

The first important thing that you have to keep in mind is that the eyes go through the middle of the head. Although at first glance it seems incredible, eyes fall half-way between the top of the head and the tip of the chin. This has to do with what we just said about the importance of information we place on the eyes, we all have a tendency to ignore the top of the head where "there is nothing except the forehead and hair".

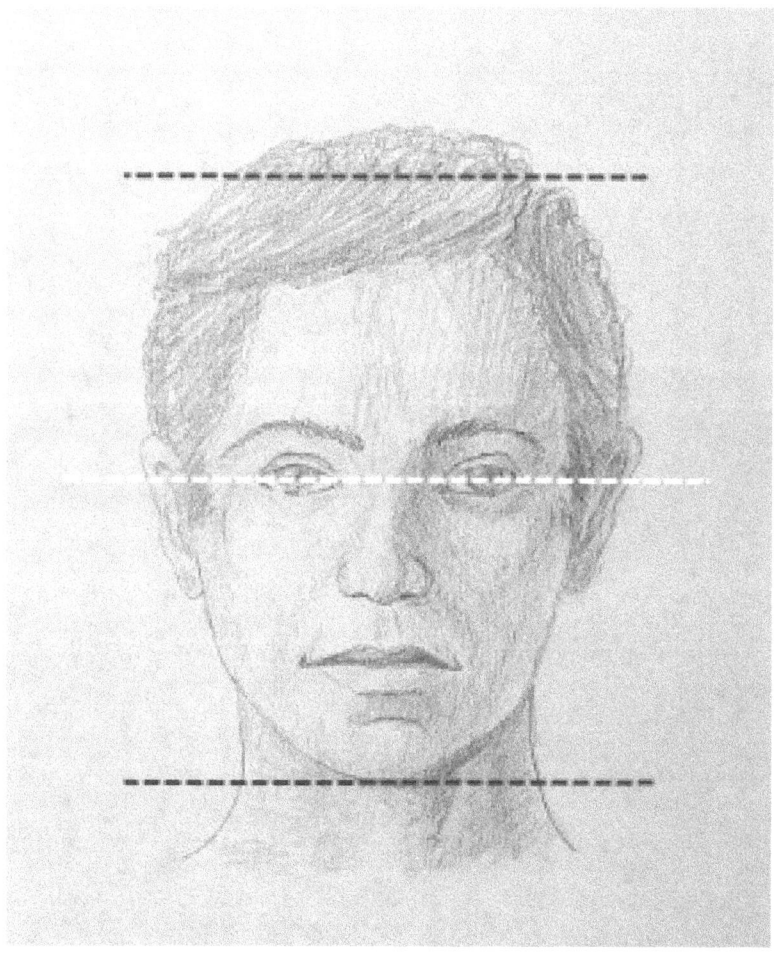

Just as with the proportions of the body, the following are guidelines to consider when drawing a portrait:

- The height of the head, from the top of the skull to the tip of the chin, is seven measures, that is, the length of the eye.

- The top of the head actually lands just below the top of the hair.

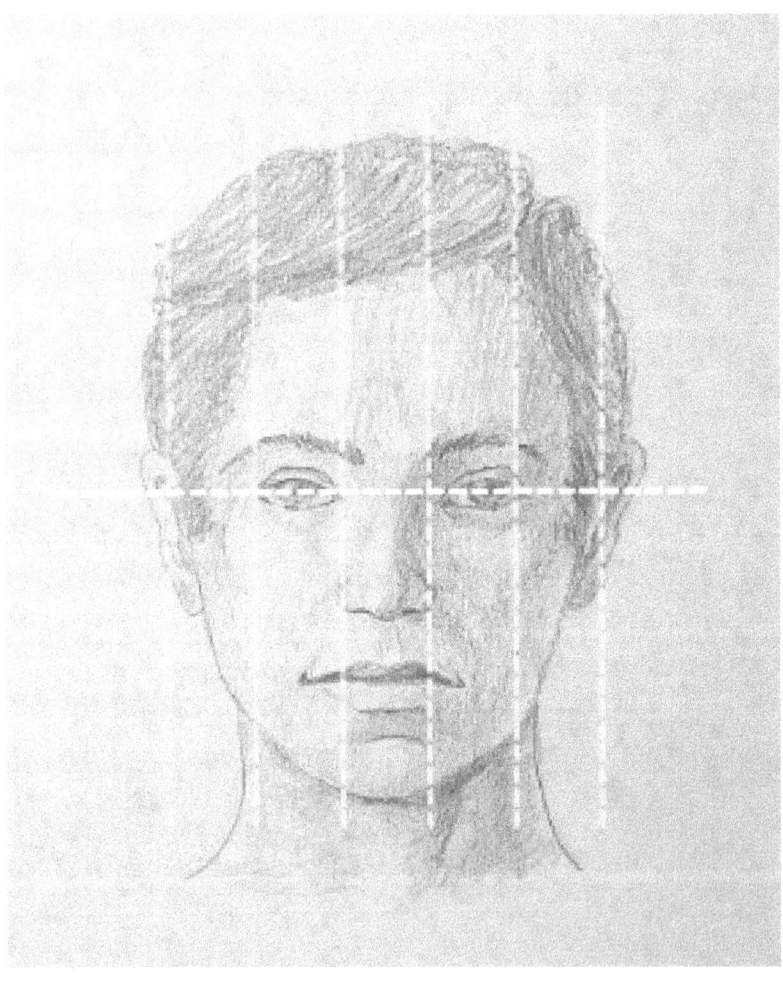

- The head is widest at about two measures from the top of the head.

- Eyebrows are roughly three measures below the top of the head. Women's eyebrows are slightly higher than men's.

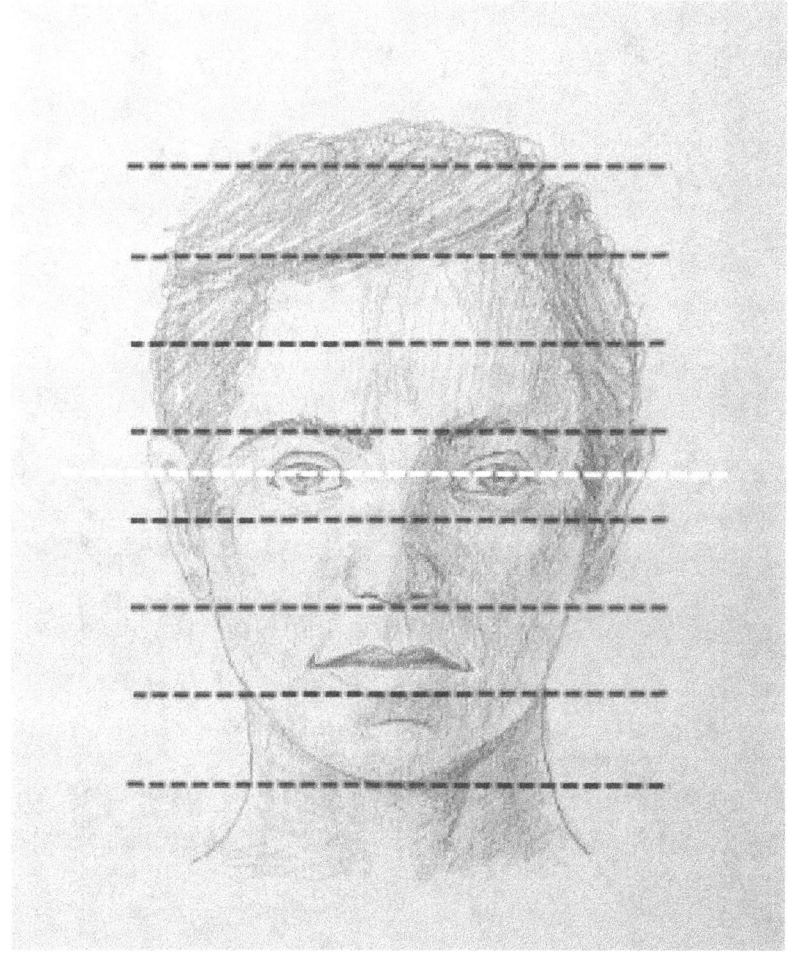

- The root of the nose starts on the line of the eyebrows, ending two measures below. From the root to the base of the nostrils the nose is two measures.

- Ears are two measures long. The top of the ears coincide with the line of the eyebrows and end on the same line where the nose ends.

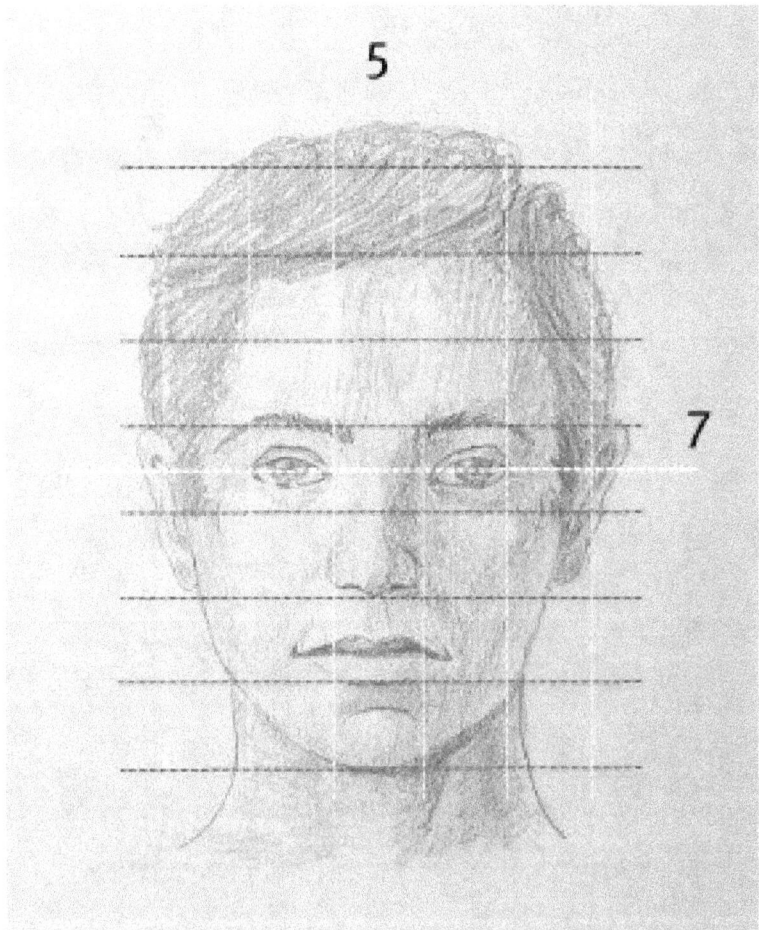

- The lower edge of the lower lip is the one measure above the tip of the chin.

- The widest part of the head is two measures under the top of the head and the head is exactly five measures across.

- The space between the eyes is equal to one eye length, measured from corner to corner.

- In its broadest part, the nose is one measure across and is aligned with the vertical lines at the inside corners of the eyes.

- The width of the neck is around 3 measures and aligns with the vertical lines at the outer corners of the eyes. In men the neck often exceeds the limits of these lines.

Although there is other more accurate, and more complex schemes used in drawing portraits anfas, this scheme is the ideal combination of accuracy and simplicity. All you need to remember is that this net of 7x5 measures and, as you will see, this same principle is also used in drawing portraits in profile.

Exercise!

On a blank sheet of paper, draw a grid of 7x5 squares. If you want the net to be perfectly accurate, then feel free to use rulers and triangles to draw them. Then, following the tips in this chapter, draw all the features of a person's head according to the set proportions. Once you are sure that you have memorized where all the features stand on the face, you can use one of the alternative methods. Regardless, the ratio of the proportions remains the same.

Chapter 5 – How to Draw with a Mannequin

If you wish to master figure drawing, you should first practice by drawing a mannequin. A mannequin is good for practicing for two main reasons. The first one is that it is something between a basic stick figure and a realistic human figure. The other reason is that it allows you to practice drawing different poses.

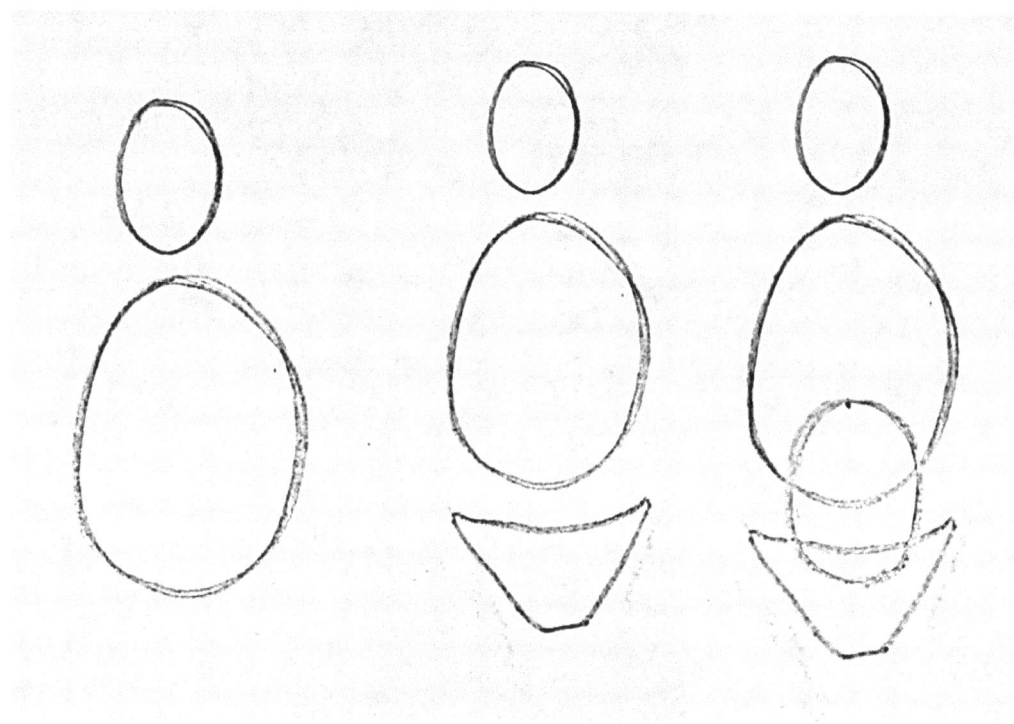

First, you will draw an oval which will represent the head, and another larger oval which will represent the torso. Next, you will draw a triangular shape for the pelvis. Afterwards, you will draw another oval connecting torso and pelvis.

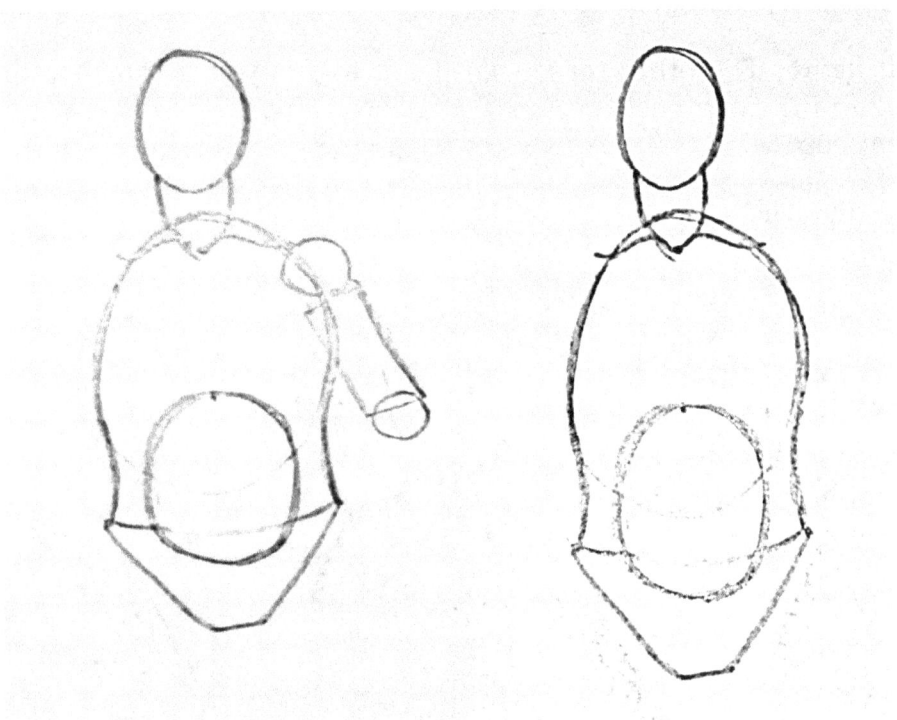

Then, draw two lines that will represent the sides of torso. Next is the neck; elongate two lines into the chest and connect them. Then draw two slightly curve lines as on the second picture below. Begin drawing arms by drawing a circle (sphere) at the top of the arm (it will be a joint-a shoulder).

Afterward, draw a cylinder which will represent the upper arm and then again draw a sphere (it will be an elbow). The sphere that represents the elbow is followed by another cylinder which tapers down towards the wrist. You can just mimic a fist by drawing a simple shape on the second picture below. Repeat the steps to draw another arm.

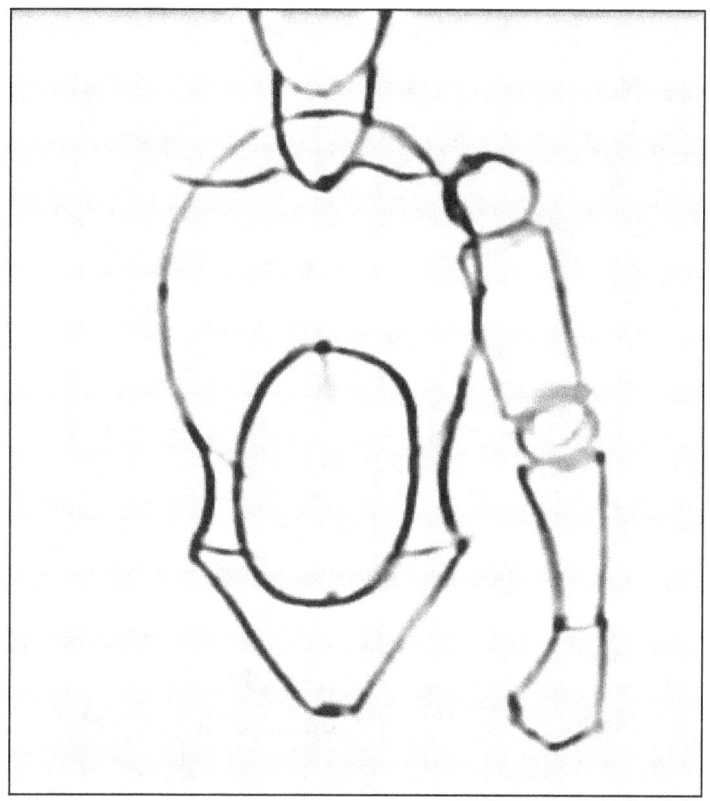

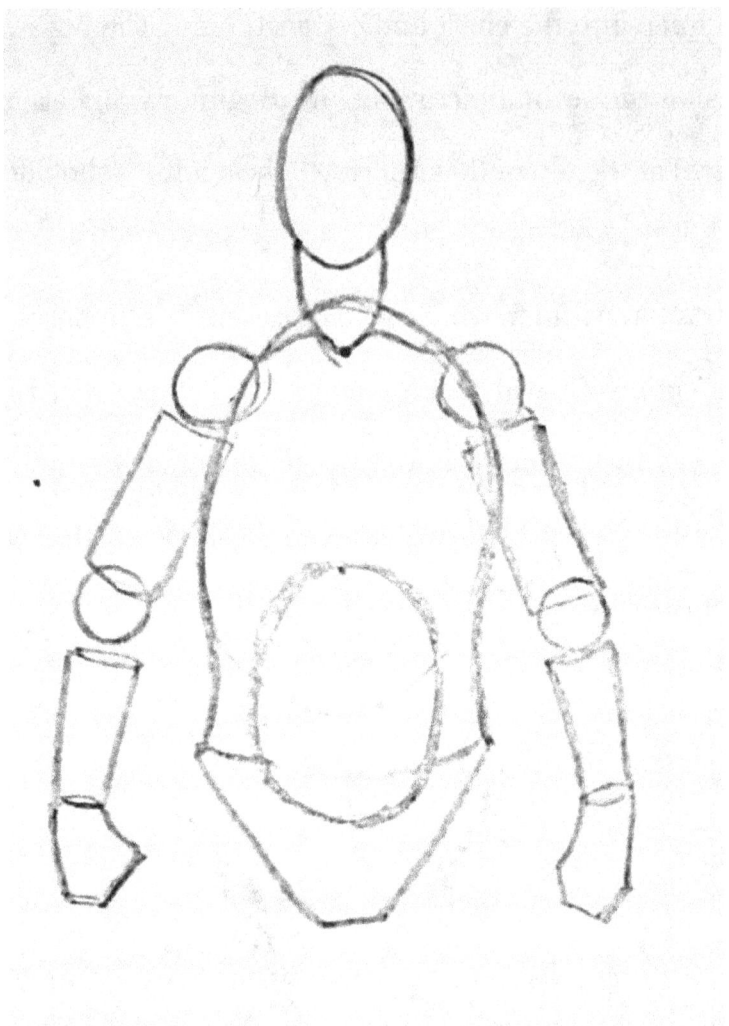

You will start drawing legs at the triangle that represents the pelvis. The external line of the thigh of the leg is a bit curved. Then draw a small cylinder, a sphere for the knee and another small cylinder. Lower part of the leg will be thinner towards the joint in the ankle which is also represented as a sphere. Simply repeat these steps for the other leg as well.

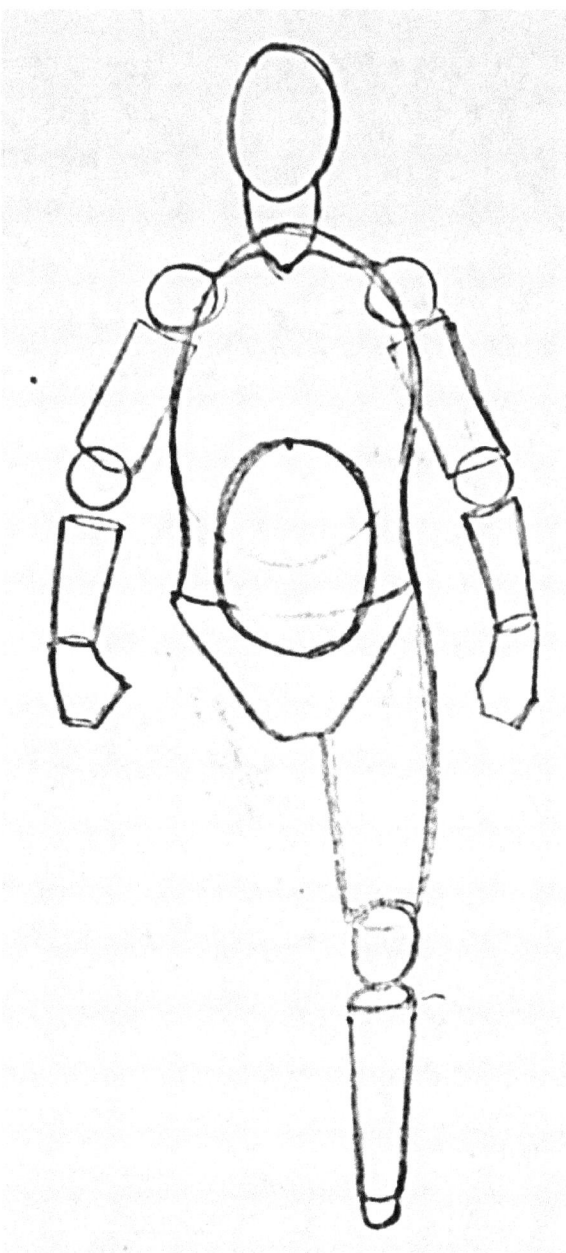

For feet you will draw a simple pyramid with a triangular base. Since we are able to see only two sides of a pyramid the feet will look this:

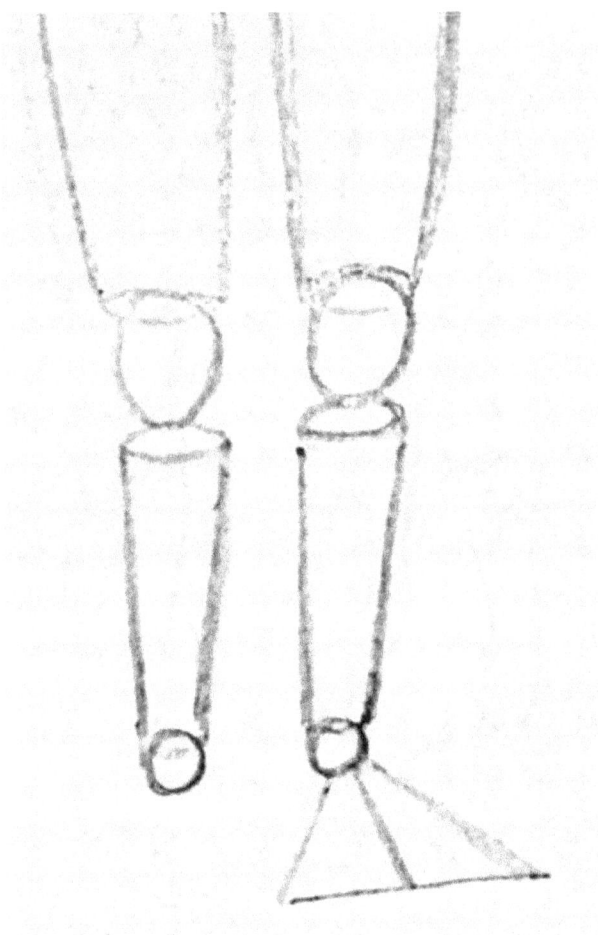

You should shade the inside of each foot. On the third picture shows the finished drawing of a mannequin.

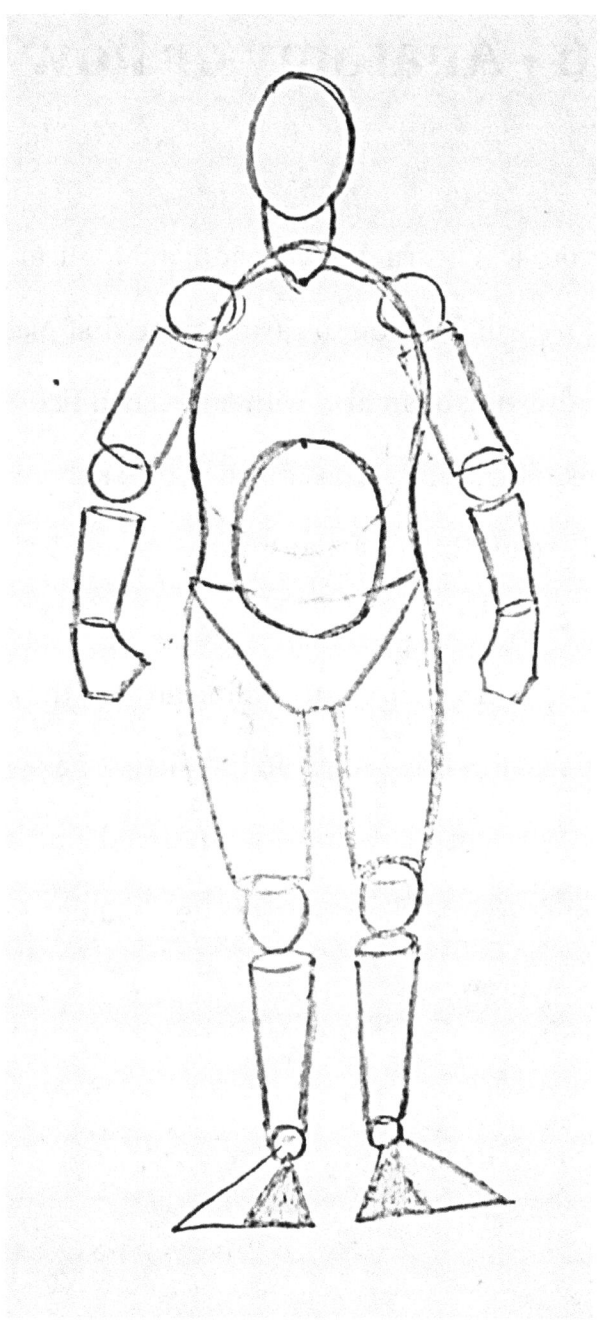

You will have to practice drawing mannequin until you feel comfortable. Also, you can practice different poses, for example, with raised arms as on the picture below.

Chapter 6 - Anatomy or how to add muscles

In this chapter you will learn how to add anatomical elements to the mannequin. First, we will focus on the arm. In the first picture shown below there is a realistic drawing of an arm with a clutched fist. To being, you will first draw a mannequin arm as we described above: sphere, cylinder, sphere, cylinder, small sphere for the wrist and simply- shaped fist.

Start at the shoulder by drawing a curved line around the circle you drew as the joint. You can see how this is done in the picture below. Next, divide the upper cylinder in two and start drawing a curved line a little above the separation point and around the inside of the shoulder joint. Connect this with the first line you drew.

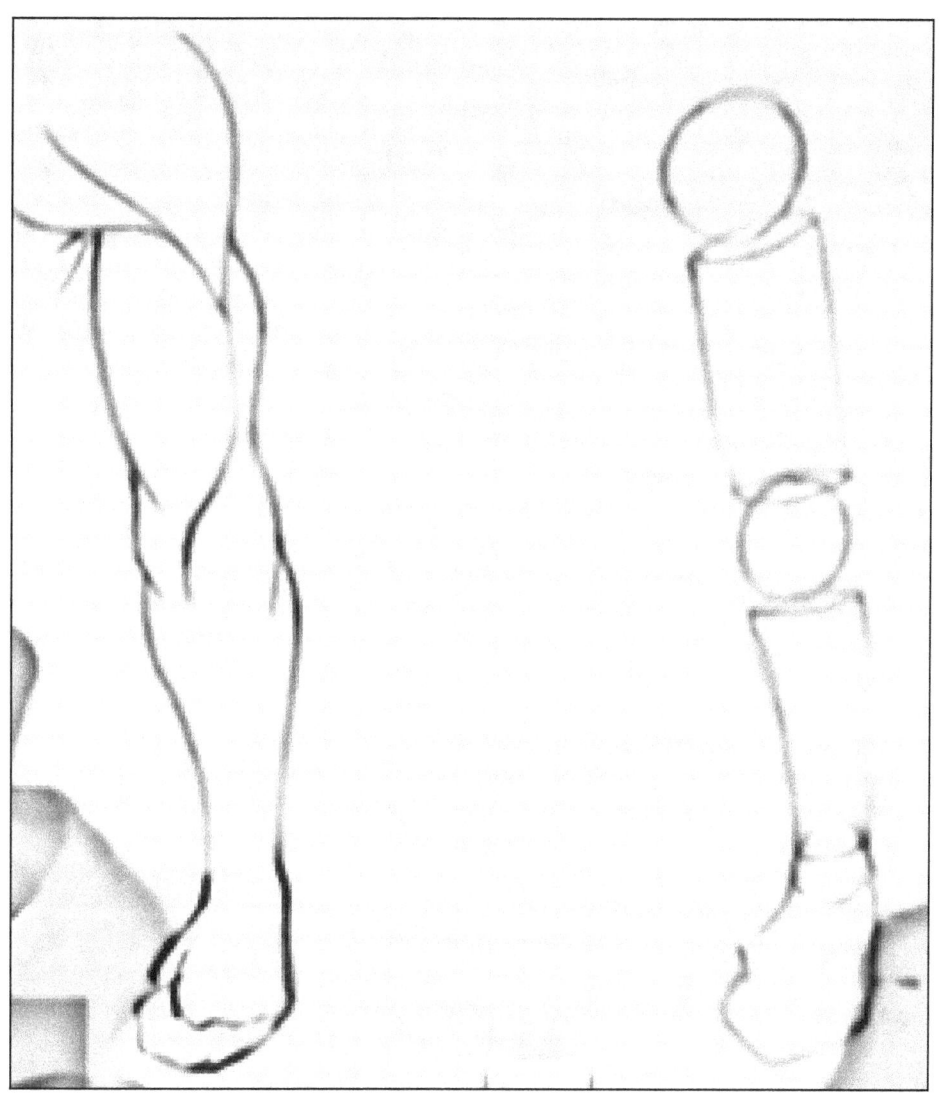

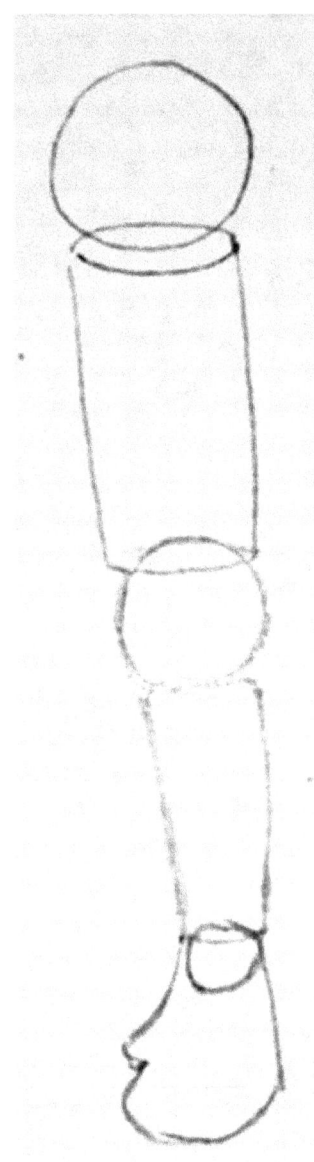

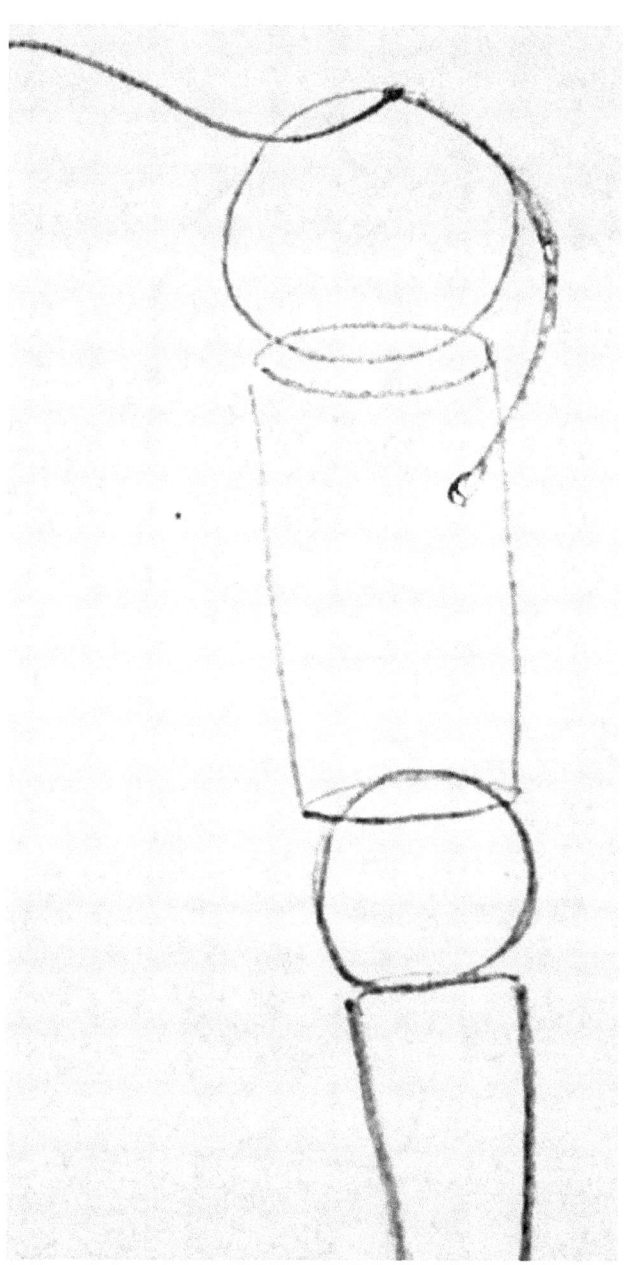

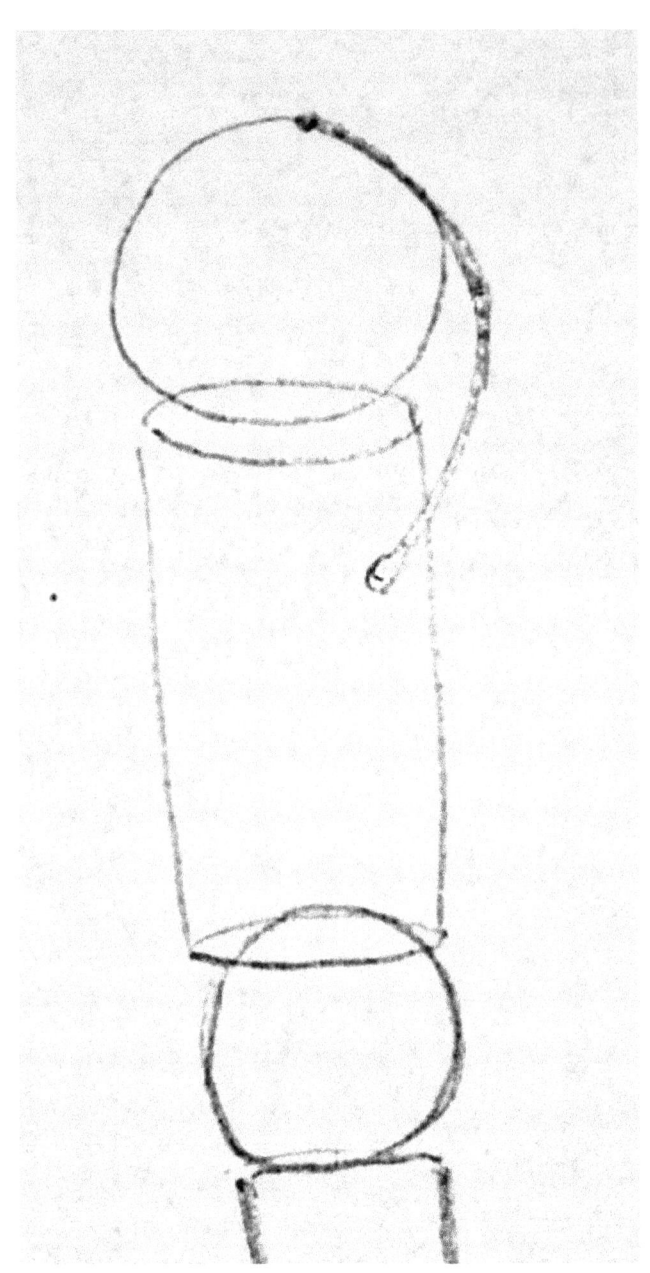

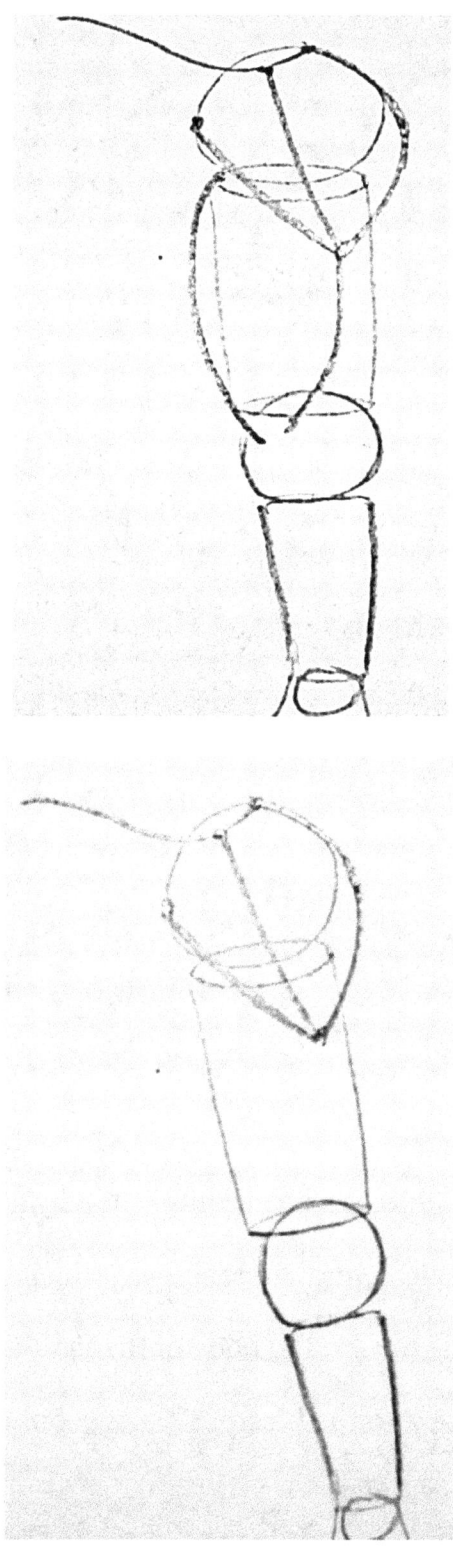

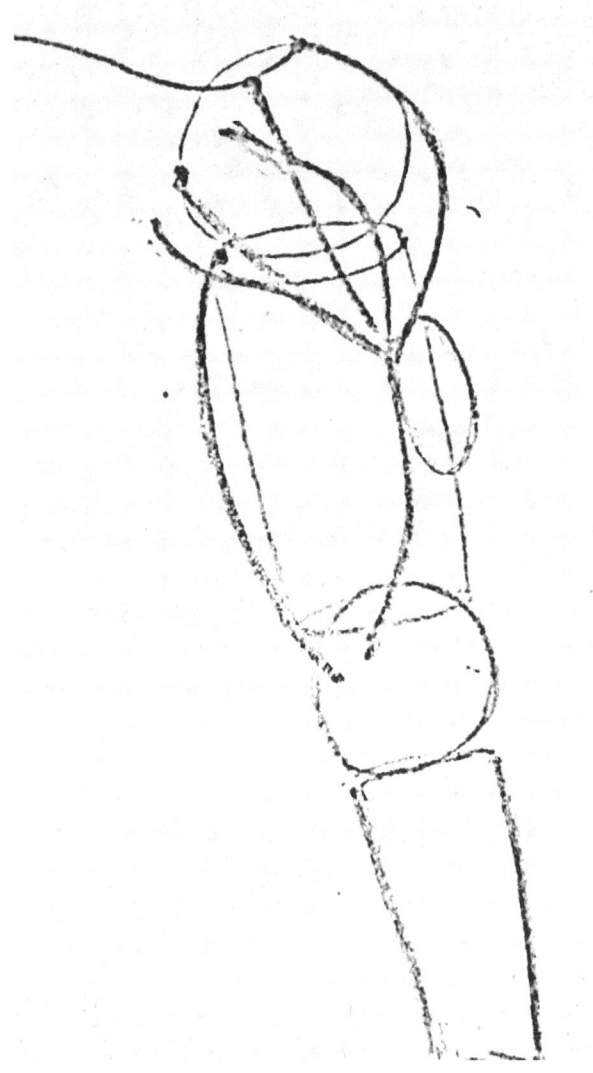

Drawing biceps and triceps can be accomplished by adding two ovals to the

top cylinder. For the bicep, draw a long oval which runs the full length of

this cylinder on the side toward the body of the figure. The triceps should be

drawn much smaller next to the bicep. This oval only needs to be roughly a

third the length of the cylinder.

Next, begin drawing the forearm. Start by drawing three ovals as on the first picture below. Then draw a 4th oval and make a line as you see in the second picture. Afterward, draw a line on the inside of the arm and erase all the lines you don`t need any more as on the 4th picture.

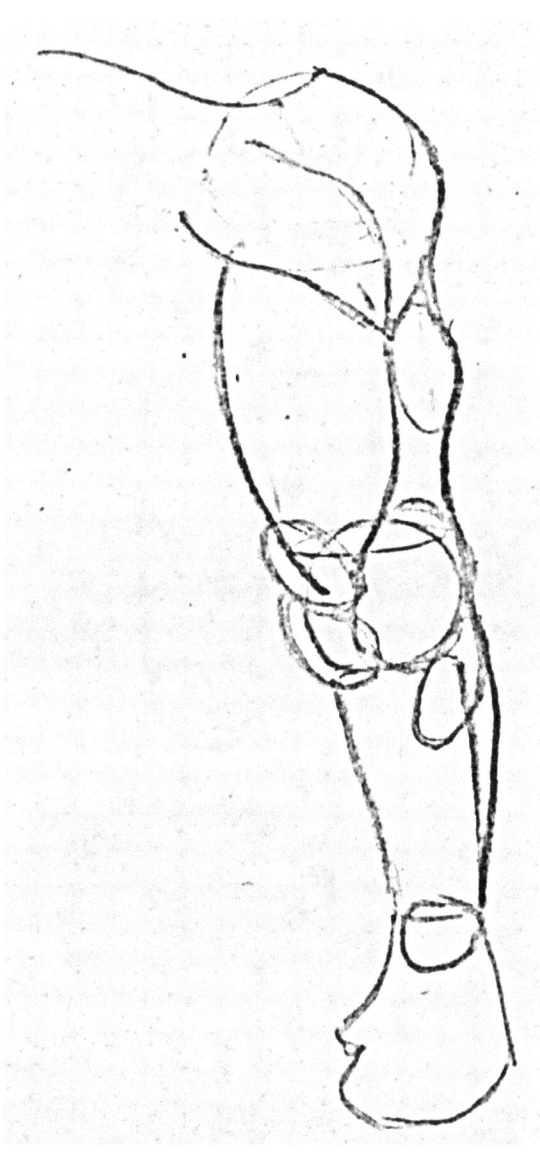

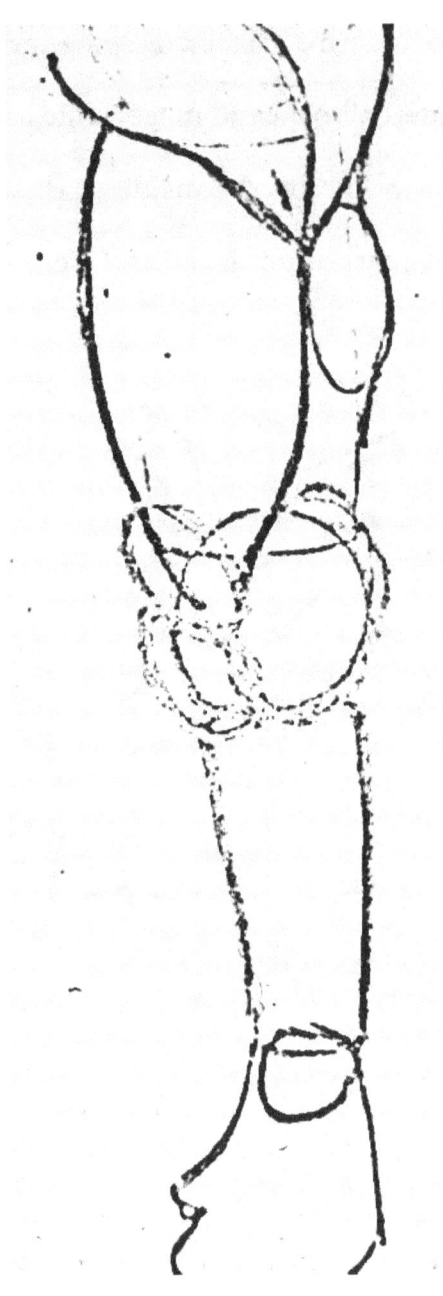

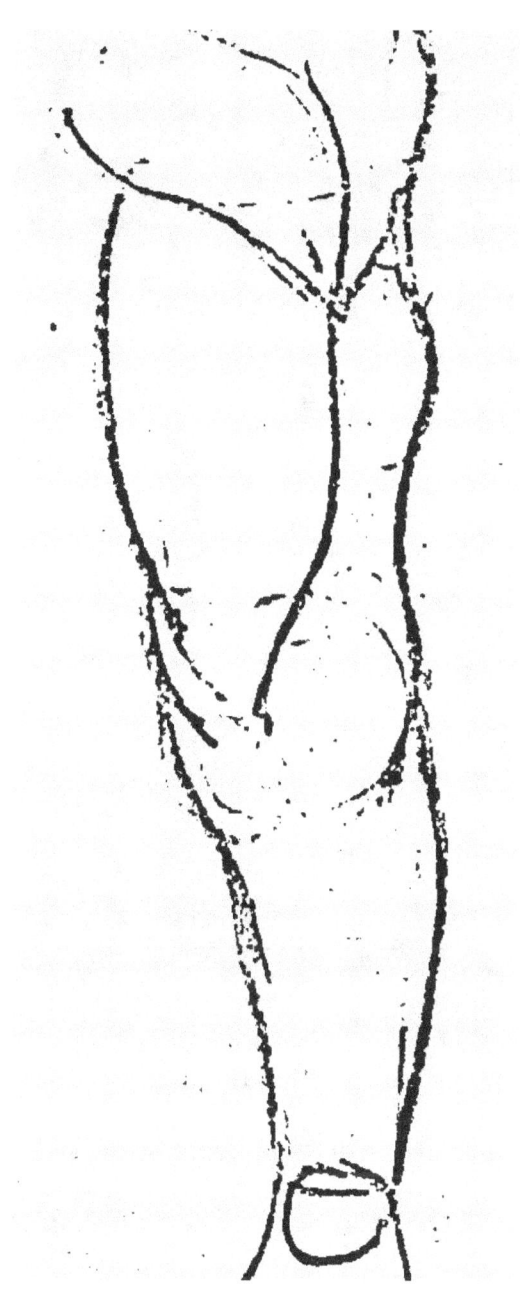

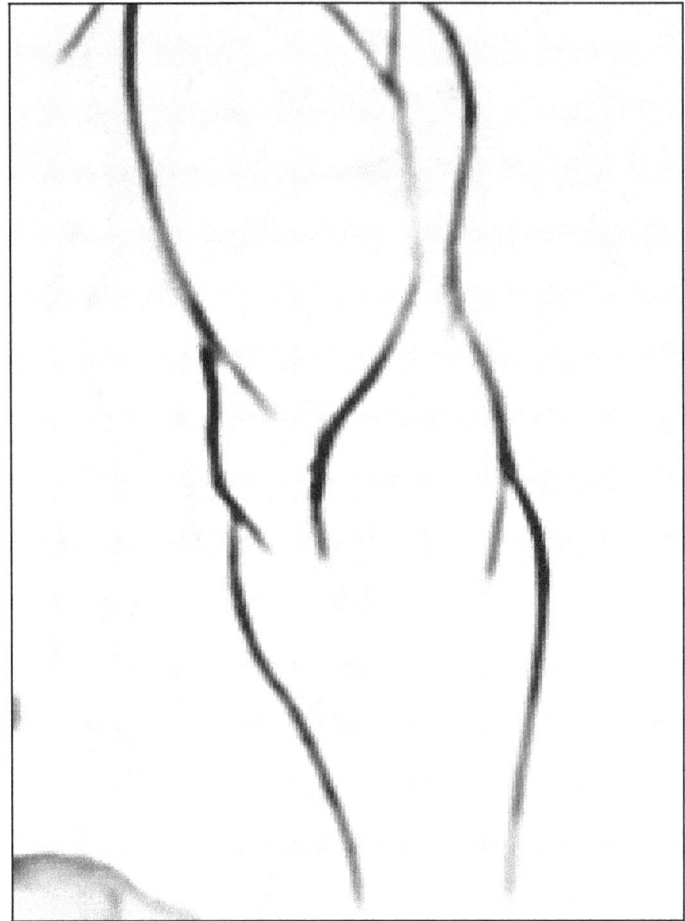

Here is some more picture guides to help you master the structure of the human body. The pictures are taken from some old newspapers. I hope they will help you. First, let`s see how to draw a masculine super hero.

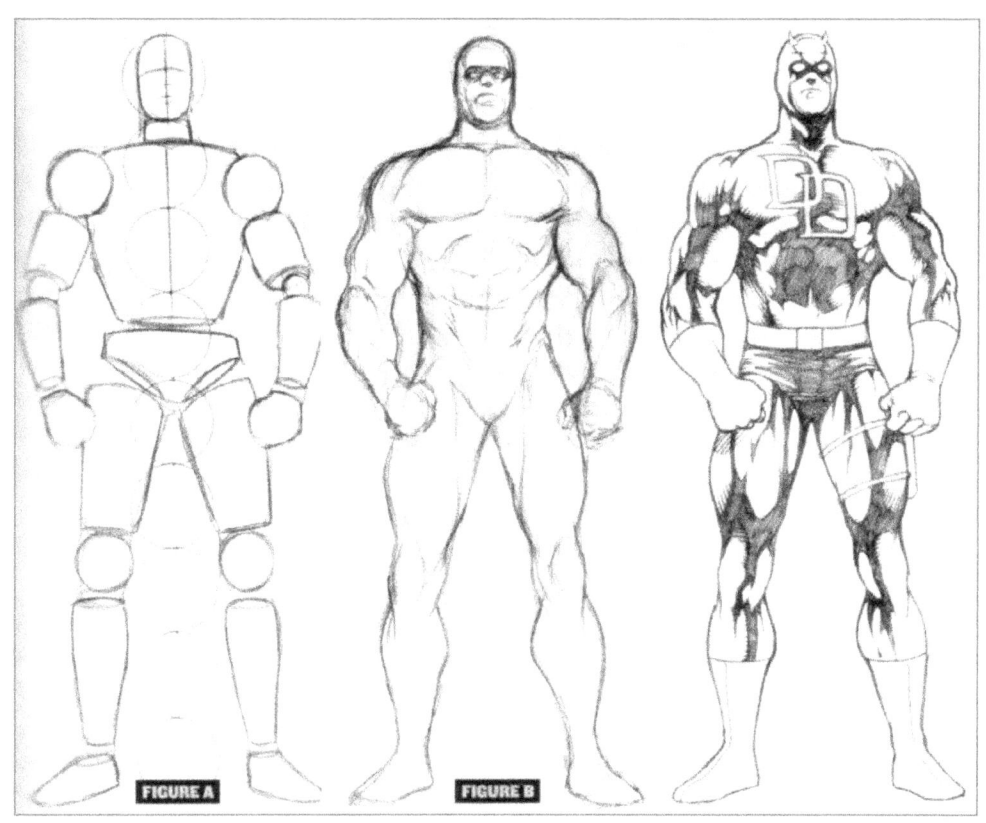

Drawing from Kevin Maquire

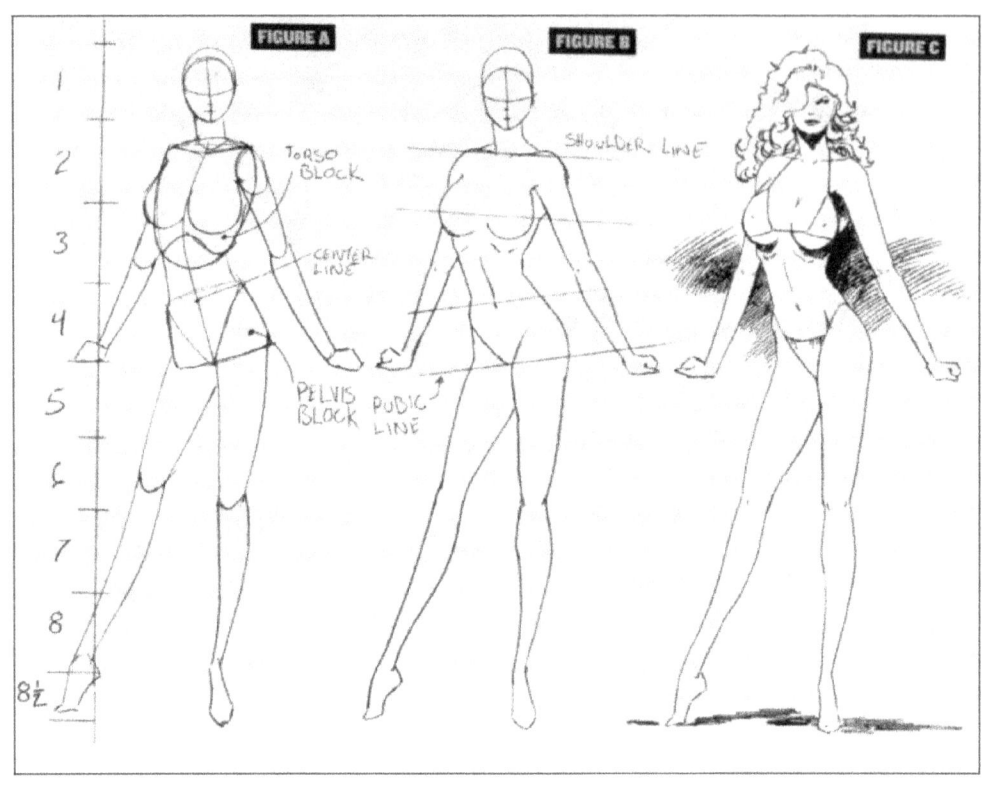

Superheroes woman by Jim Balente

Chapter 7 - Drawing poses

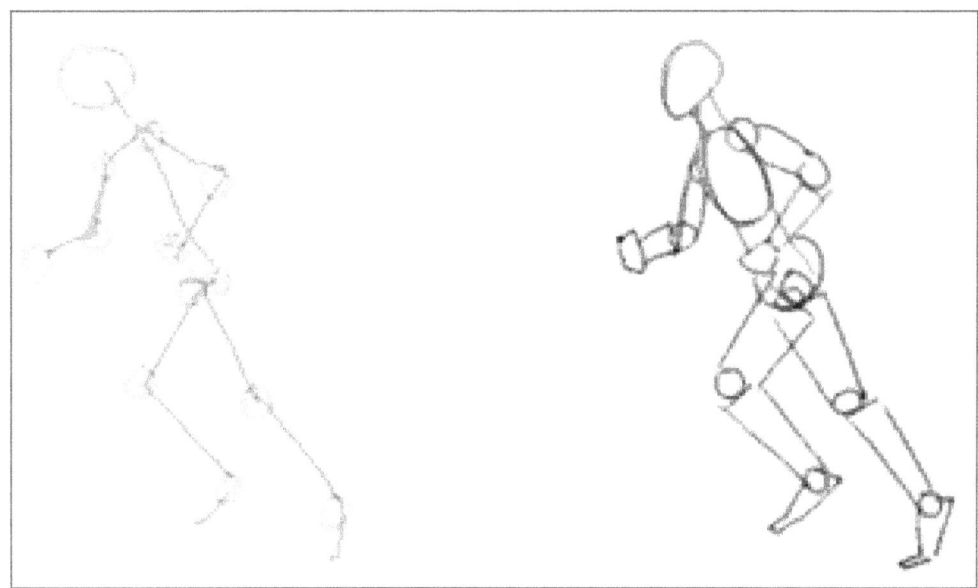

I have found what, in my opinion, is very good pictures for beginners to learn how to draw poses. As you can see in the pictures you should first draw a skeleton, then geometric shapes, and in the end you will erase all the lines you don`t need.

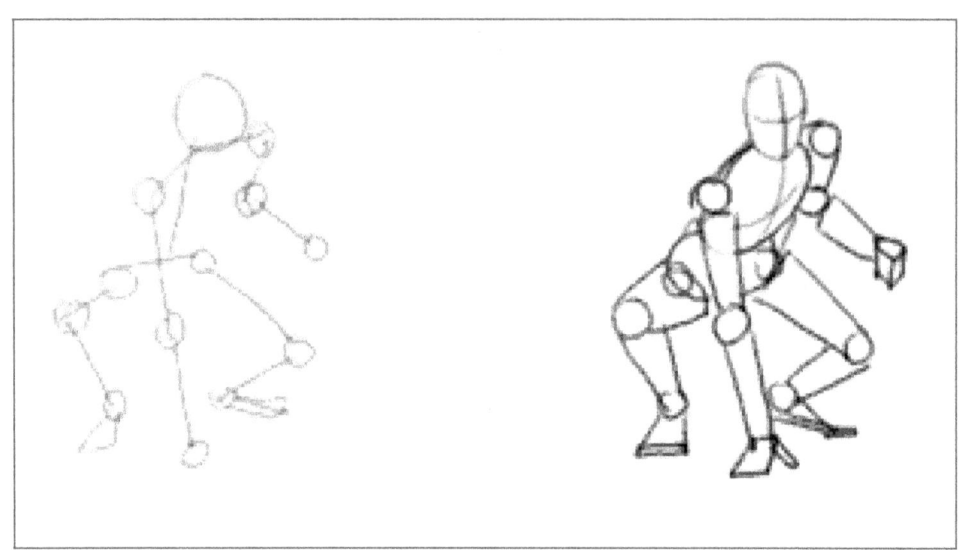

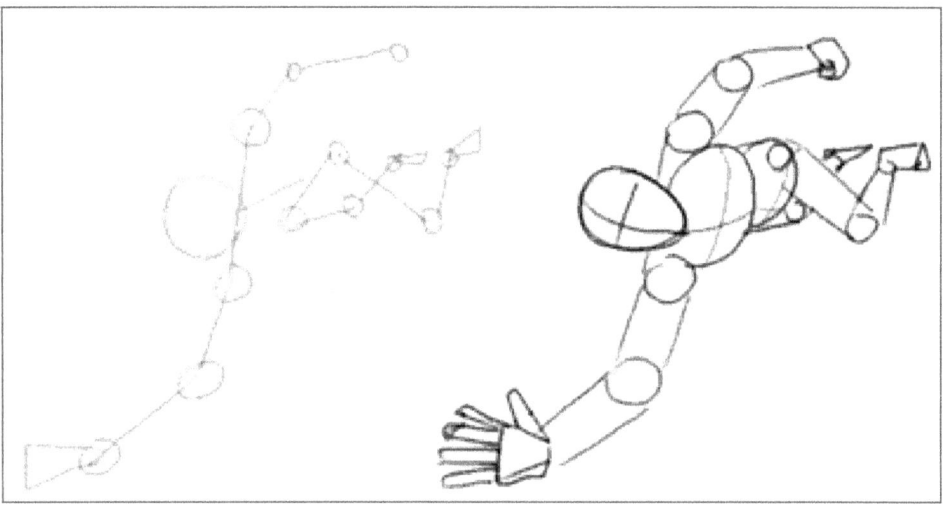

Next, I will show you how to draw different poses step-by-step. You will begin by drawing an oval for the head and then a simple stick figure as shown on the pictures below.

Picture source: elfwood

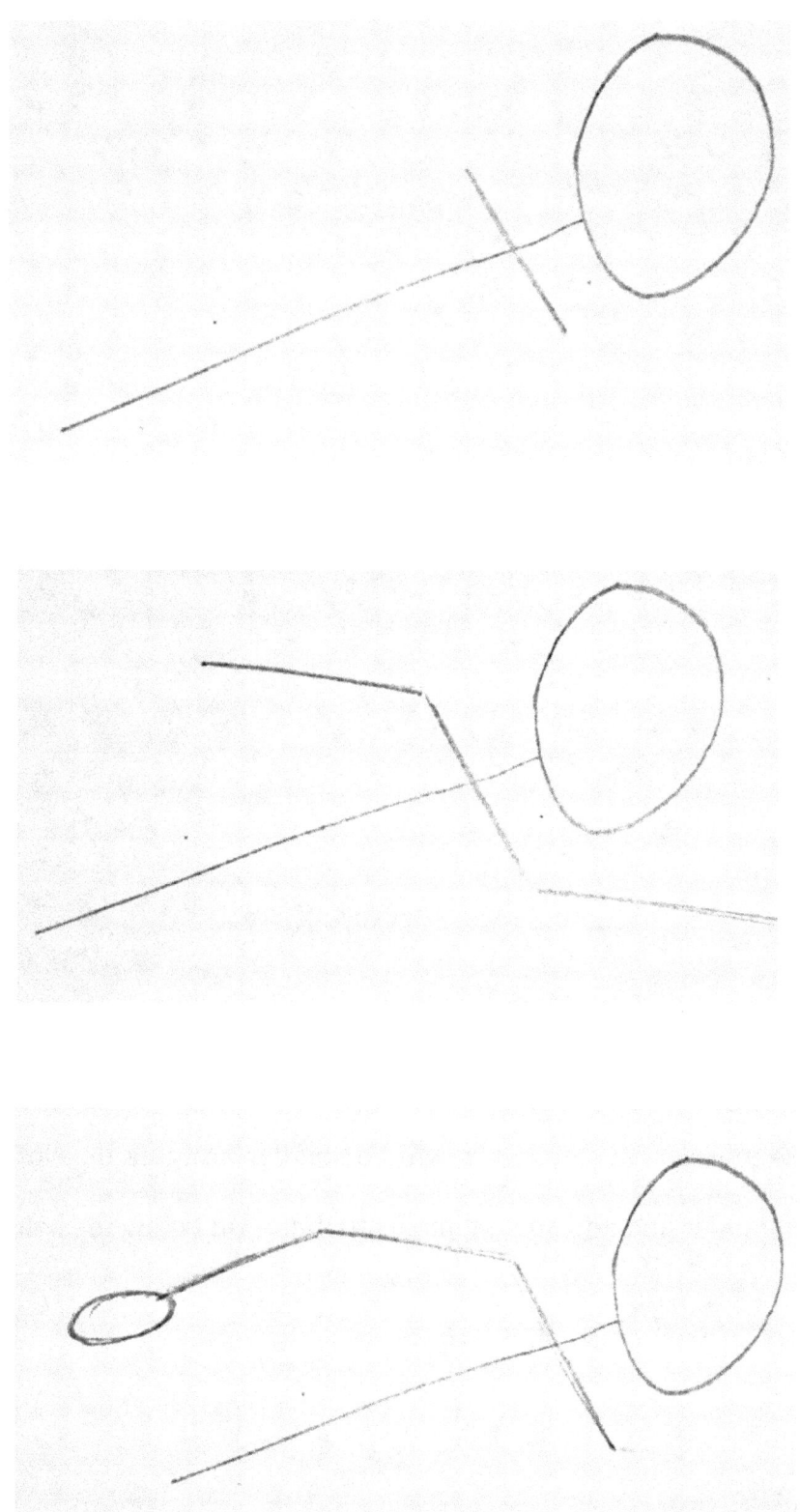

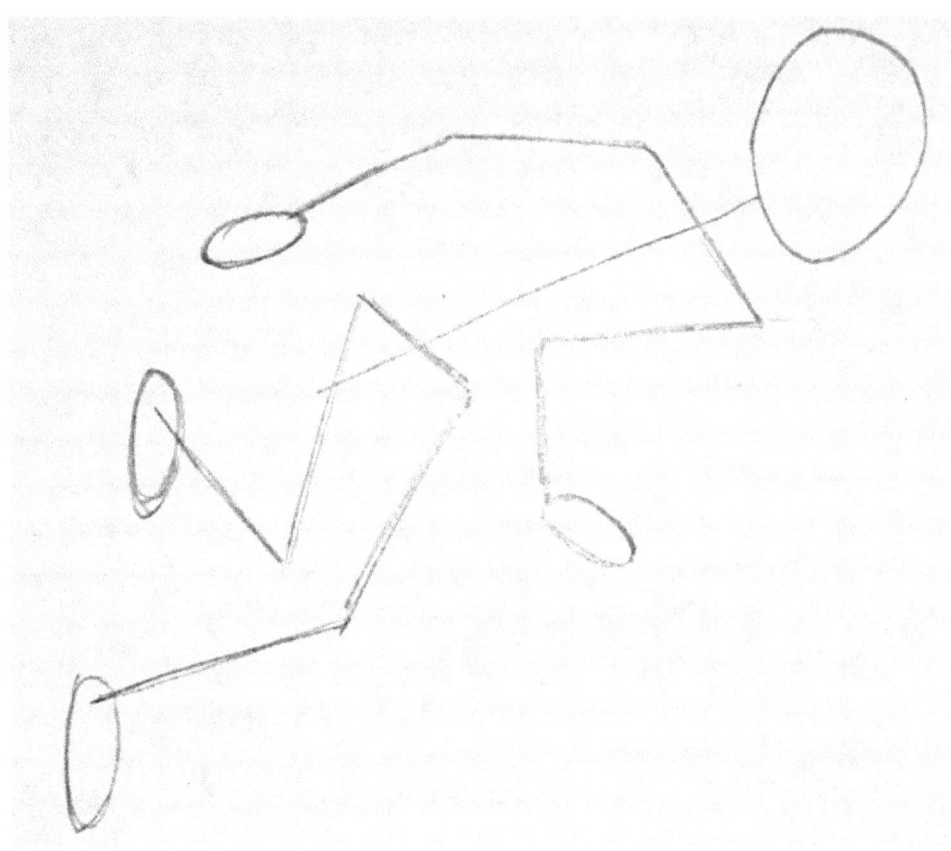

As with the arm we drew, after you have drawn a rough skeleton, you start adding muscles to it beginning from the arm and neck. As this is a female figure, the muscles on this figure will be smaller and less developed. Draw another shoulder and add some female attributes on below the belt.

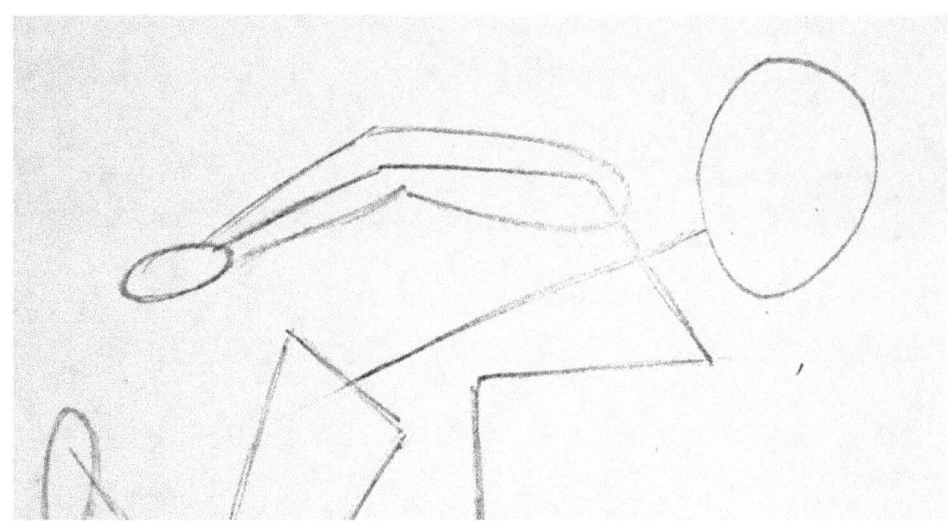

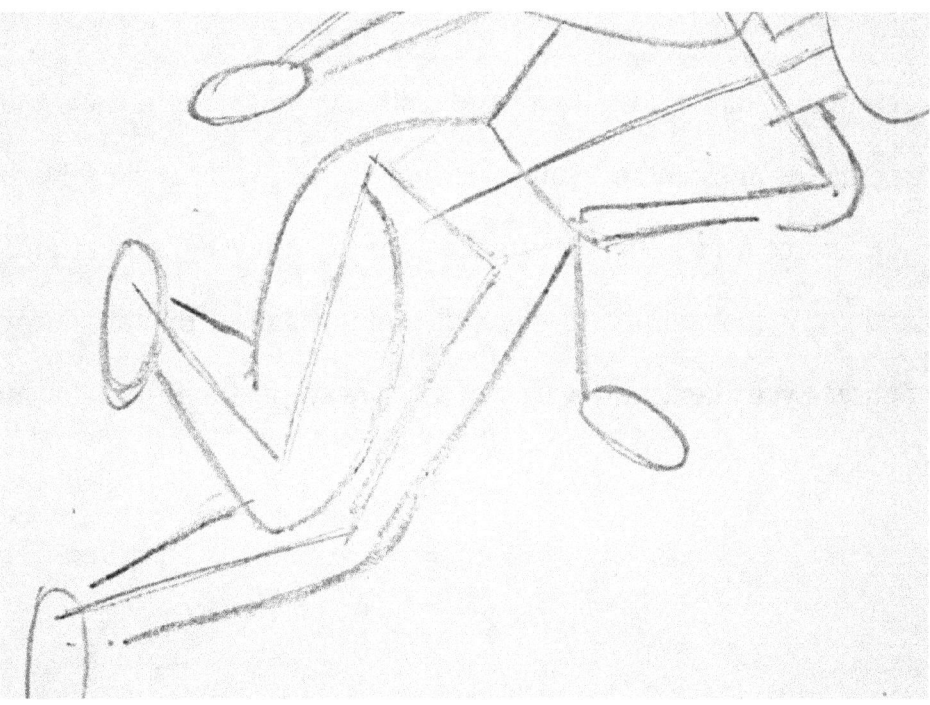

Pictured below is how to add the breasts, collar, and legs.

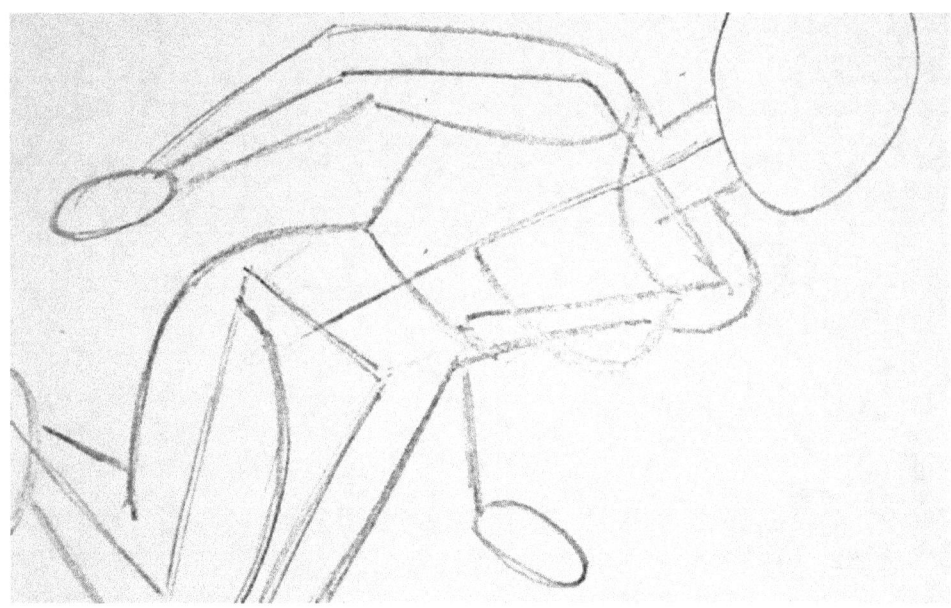

Then refine the shape of the foot. And lastly, all you have to do is to erase the stick figure lines. When you learn how to draw, let`s say, five or six different figures you will begin to be able to draw a figure from your imagination. At that point will you will no longer need to start out with a stick figure. Even then, however, you can always use it to draw a human figure, it`s very helpful.

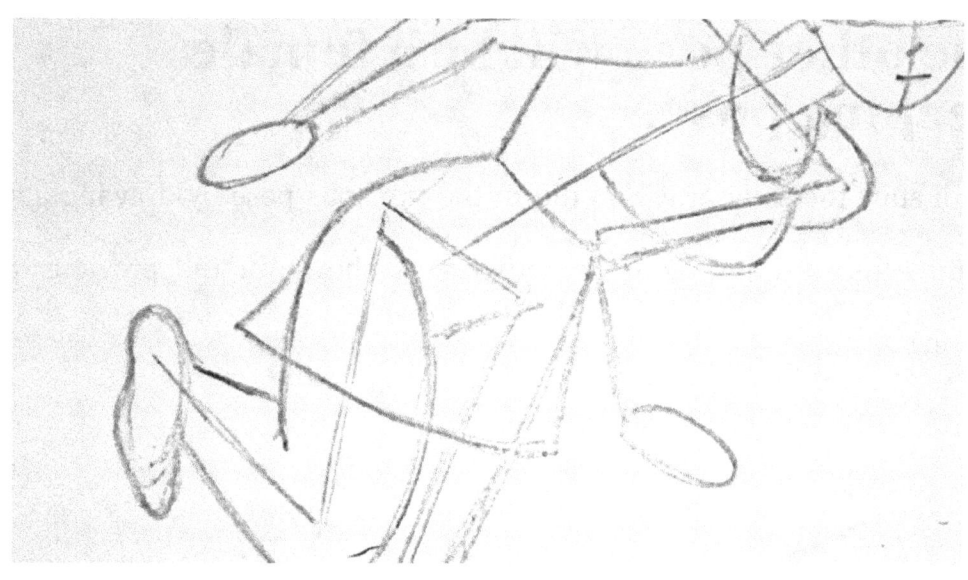

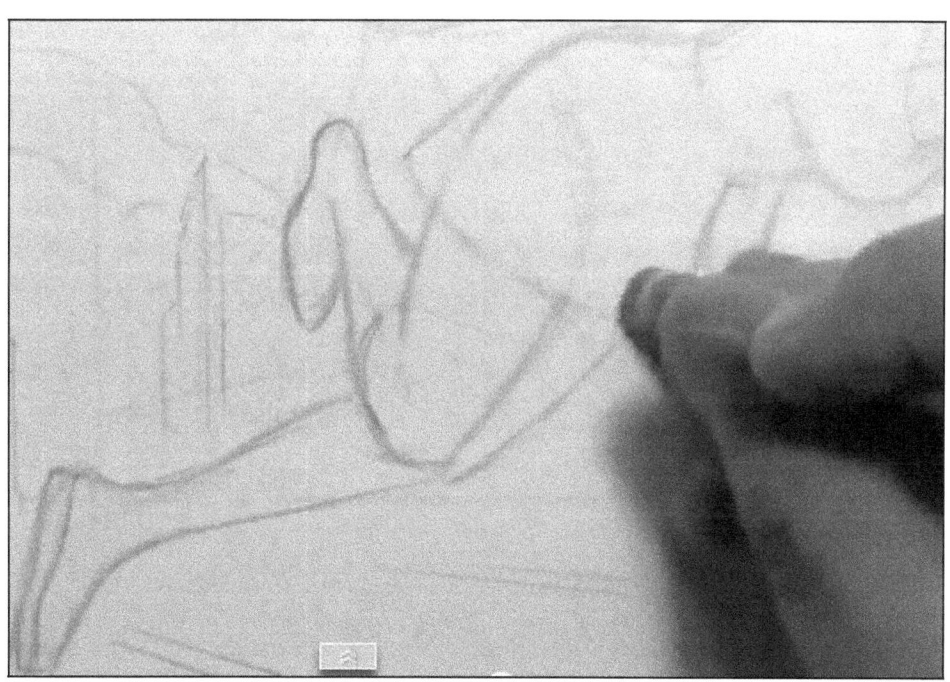

The other pose will be a female sleeping pose.

You`ll start the same way you did in the previous pose by drawing a stick figure. Afterward just add the muscles as shown in the previous pose drawing.

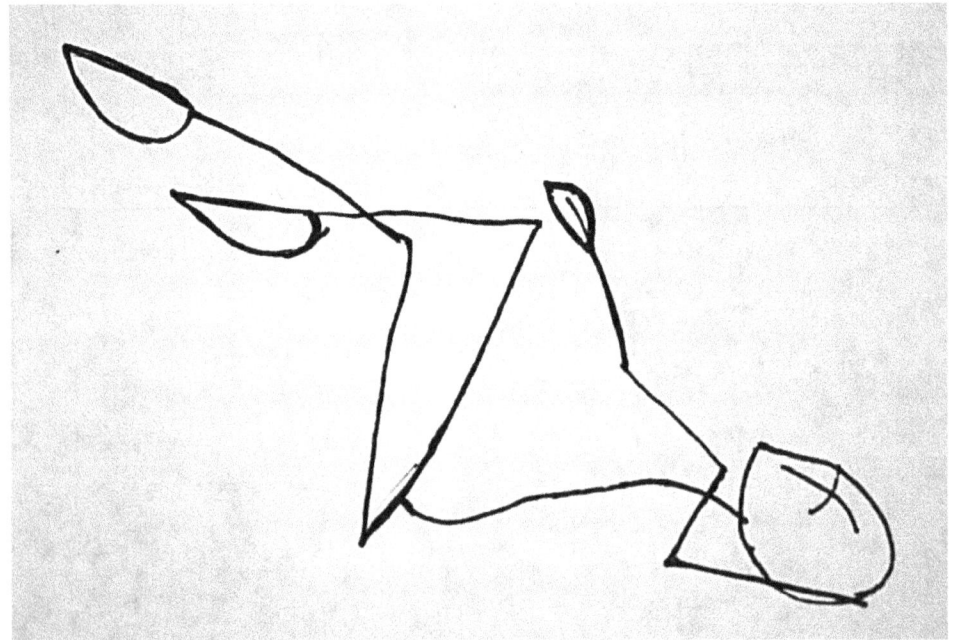

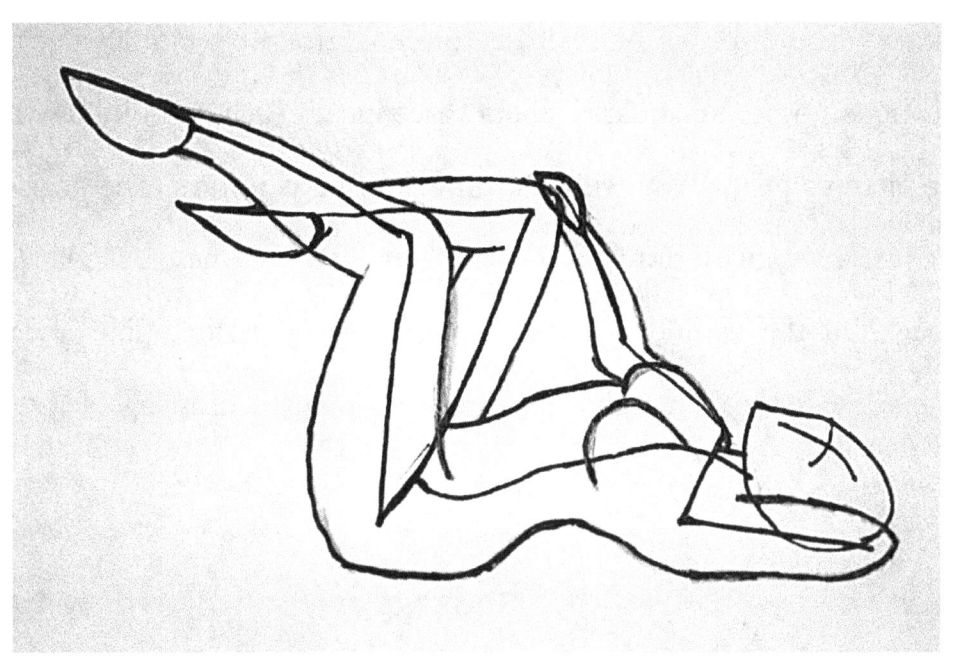

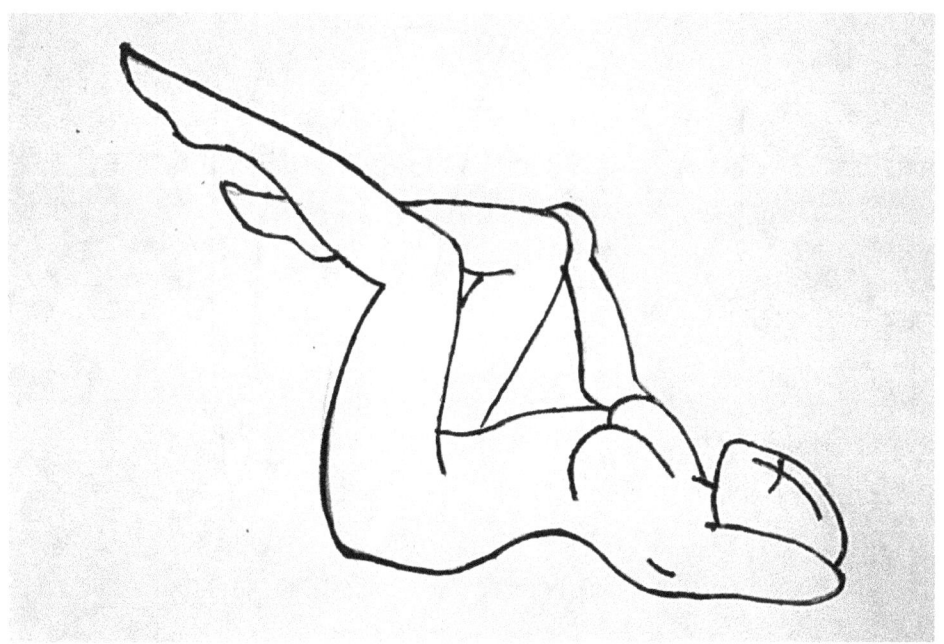

Next, you can draw a man sitting on the ground by following these instructions. Draw two squares, about three inches each and fill it as shown in the pictures below. You will first draw a head as always. The horizontal line is just a help with drawing the shoulders and the line on the left is for the back. In the second picture you will see something like a curved rectangle and in the third one you will see how to begin drawing a leg.

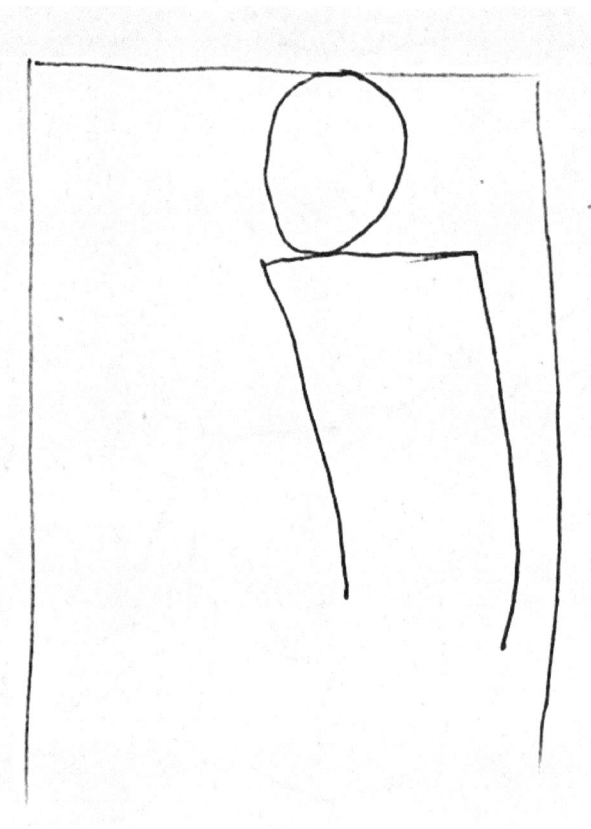

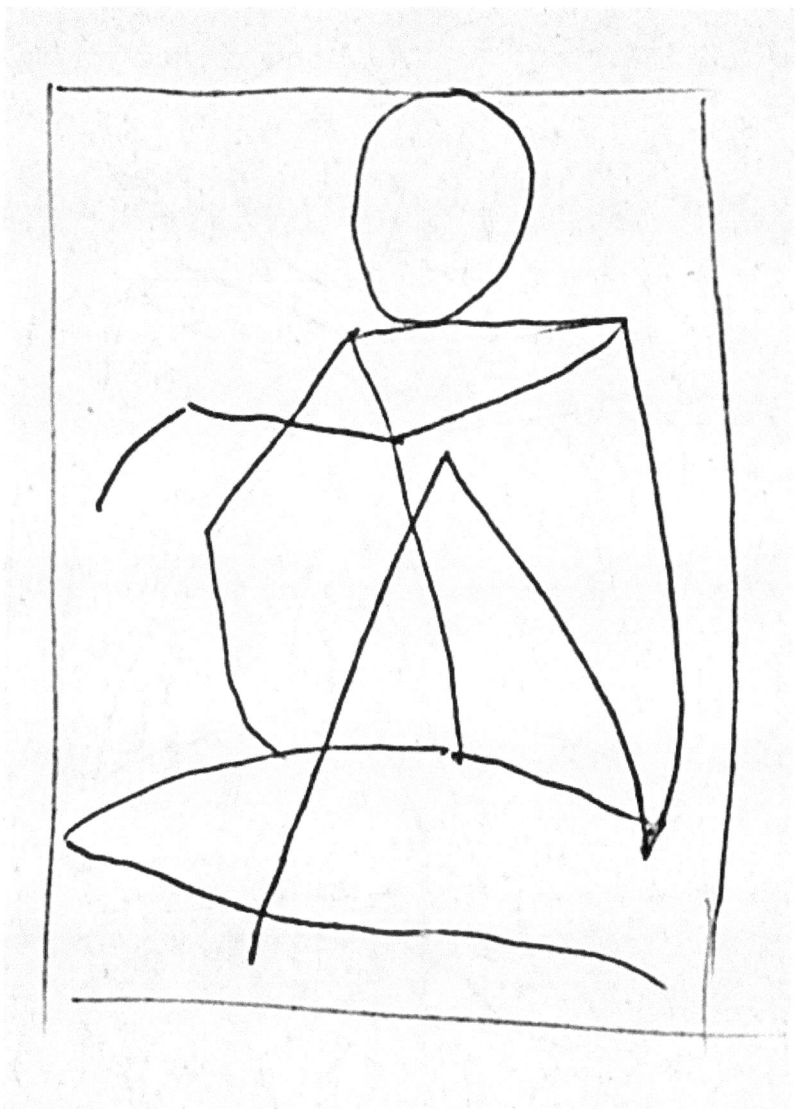

You will then draw another leg and begin drawing an arm. On the third picture below you can see you have to curve those straight lines a bit so it looks more realistic.

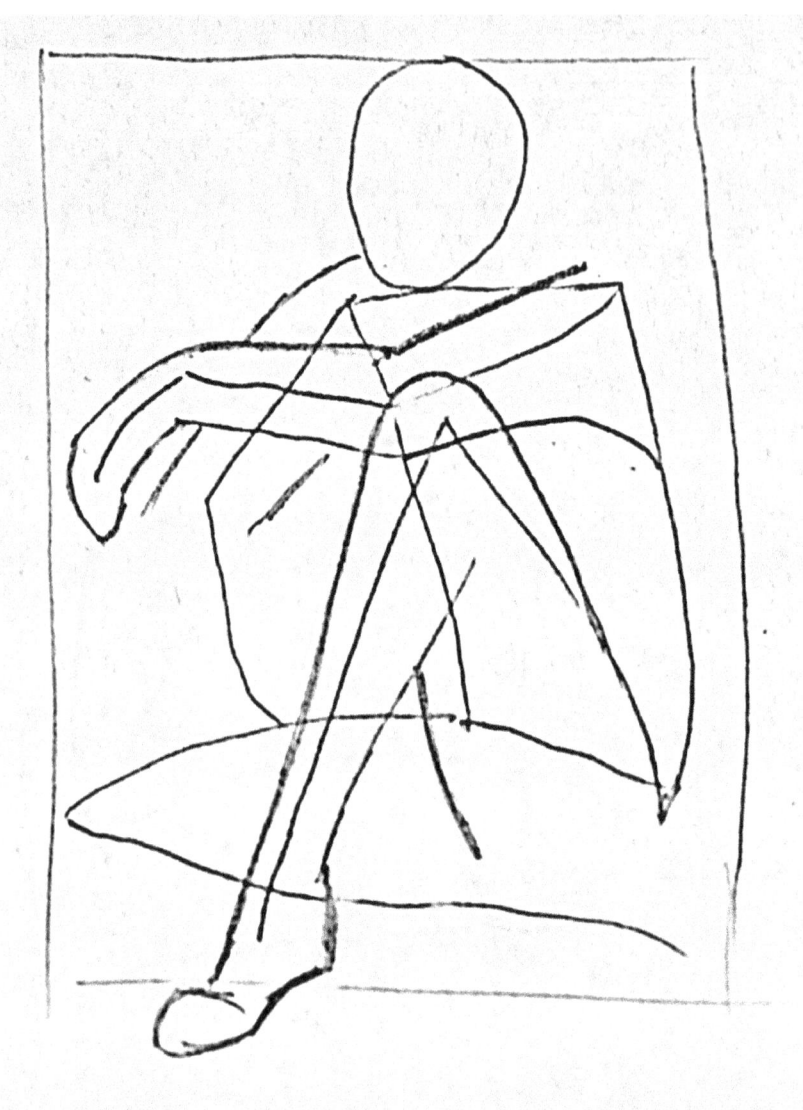

A man sitting on the ground is finished. The man looks like he is resting or thinking about something.

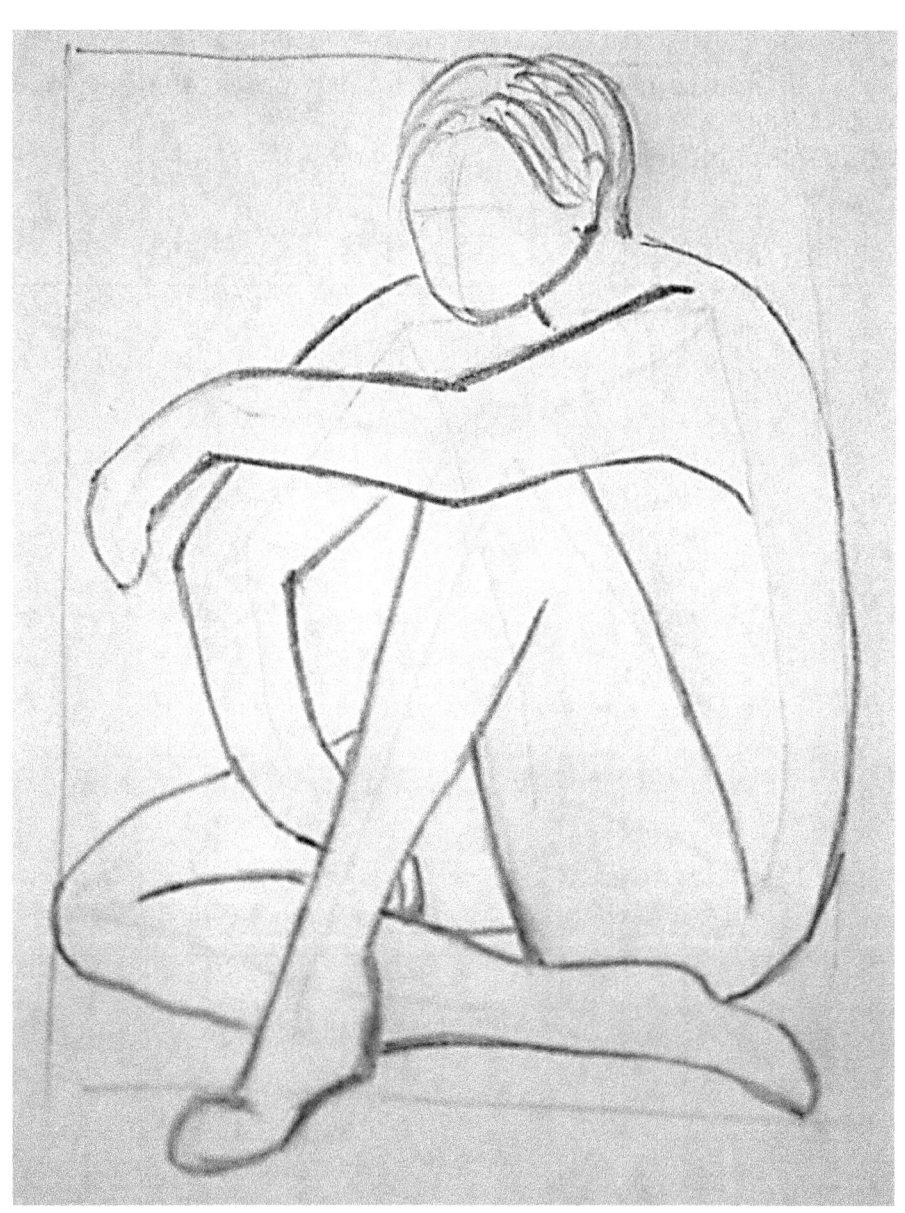

Below you can find some wallpapers of human poses, the best ones I`ve found while searching the net.

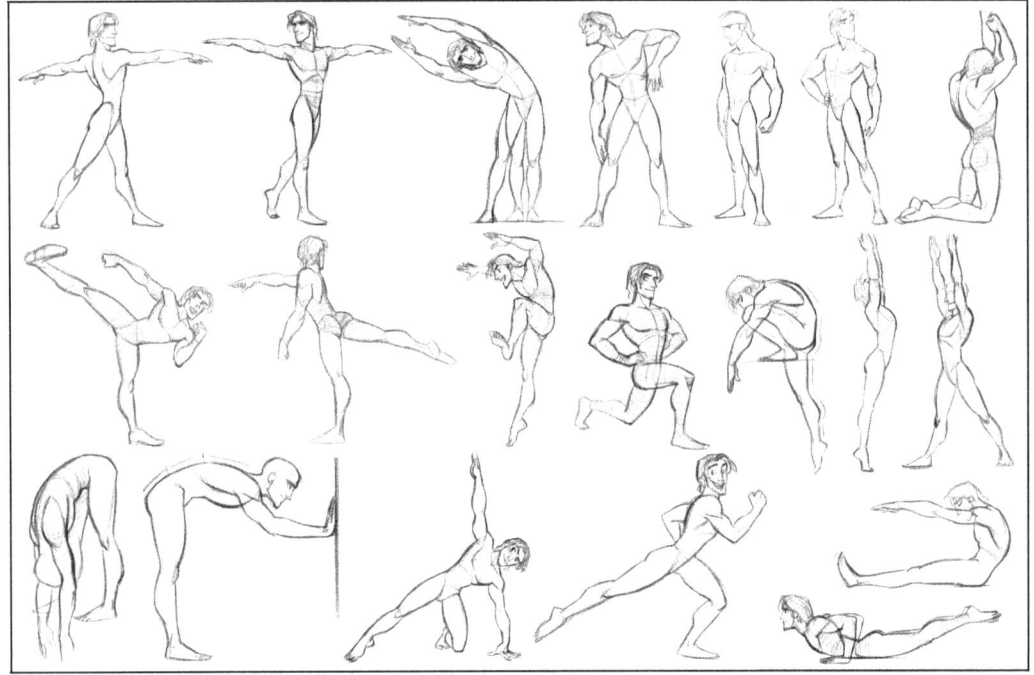

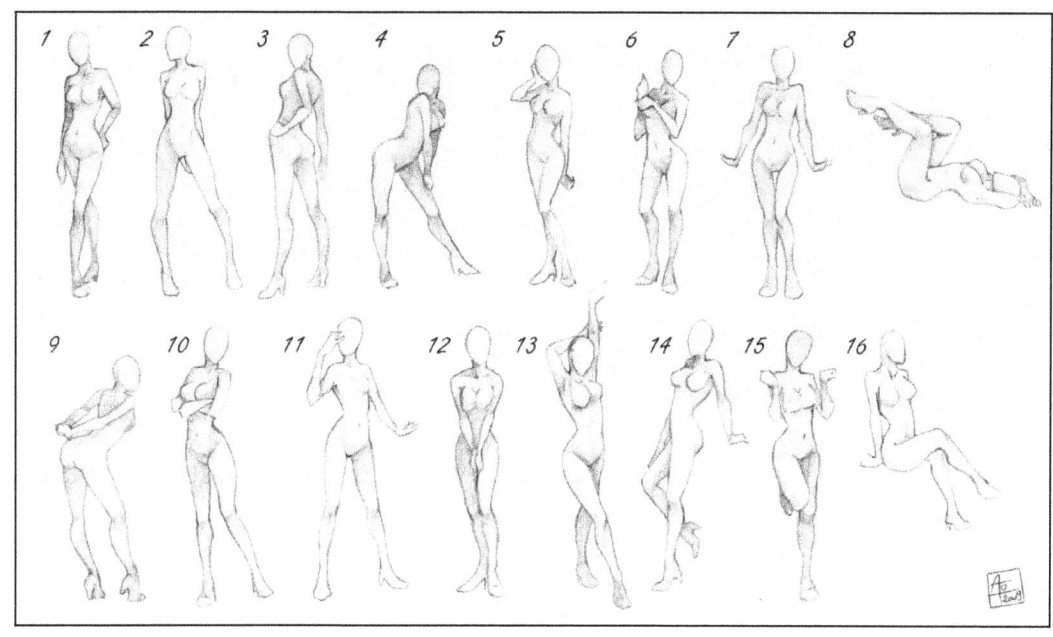

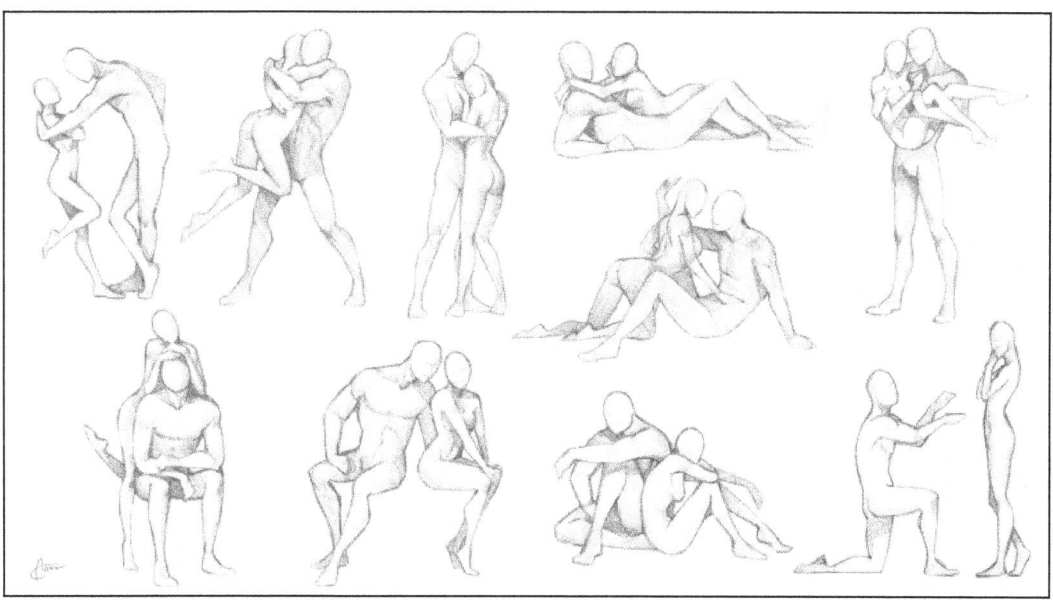

Picture source: Quick poses

Chapter 9 - Blocking-in the figure with shapes

As we discussed earlier, it can be helpful to break down a complex figure into simple shapes such as triangles and rectangles. This process, called 'blocking-in' is when you start with these general simple shapes, and gradually move towards the specific and complex shapes in a subject like the human figure, for example. Blocking-in helps by giving you the border in which you can draw the more complex shapes. You can draw anything by using this procedure.

Blocking-in also helps you imagine the entire figure and the relationship between different parts of the body. I consider blocking-in the best way to draw almost anything. You can use any of the basic geometric shapes and let your imagination run wild within this basic outline.

Basic shapes are a starting point when you begin drawing, as we've already stated in previous chapters. For example, when you look at a person, first try to identify the basic shapes which make up its form. Then, once you've drawn the basic shapes, add details little by little. By defining basic shapes of people and objects, we ascertain the general character of what we are drawing, as well as relative proportions.

Exercise!

Place yourself in front of a pair of objects and watch them. When you see the basic shape, draw them and then gradually add more details. Always add shapes in descending order. It can work with anything, from television to apples to people.

Now, we will see how to block in a figure with a triangle. You can see on the first couple picture how you can start with a triangle and then begin breaking it down into smaller shapes.

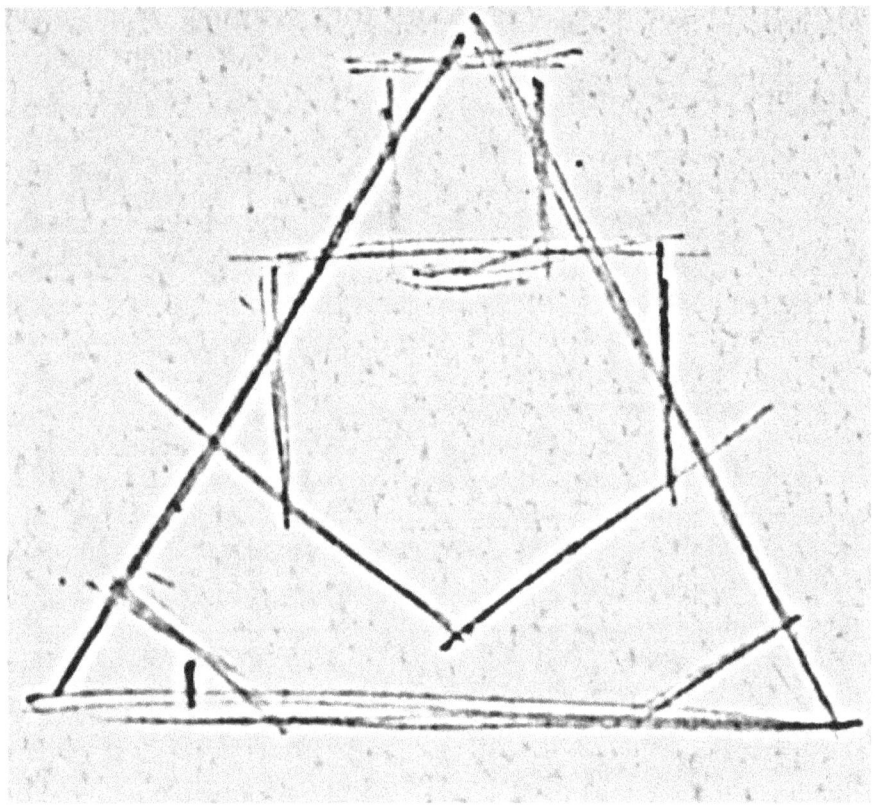

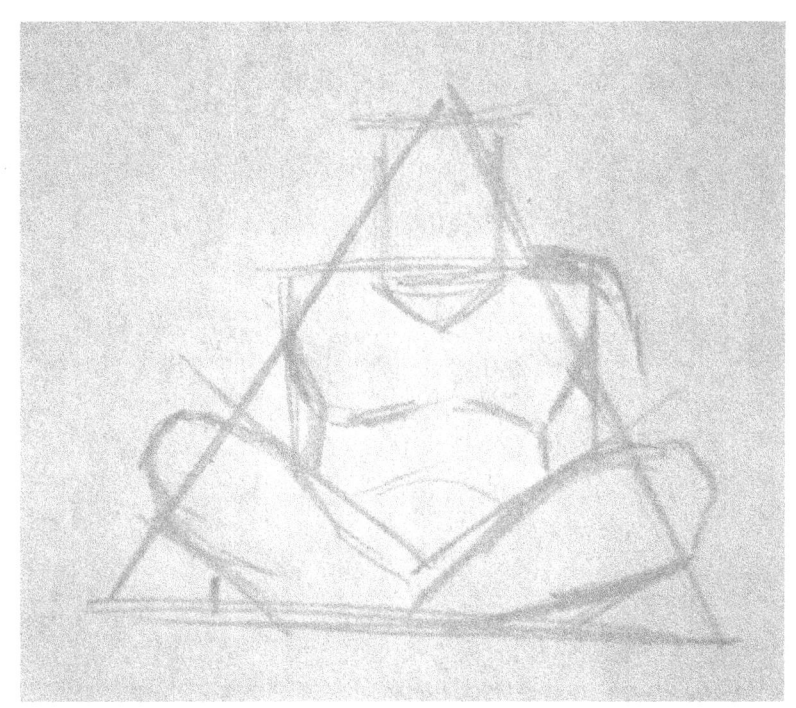

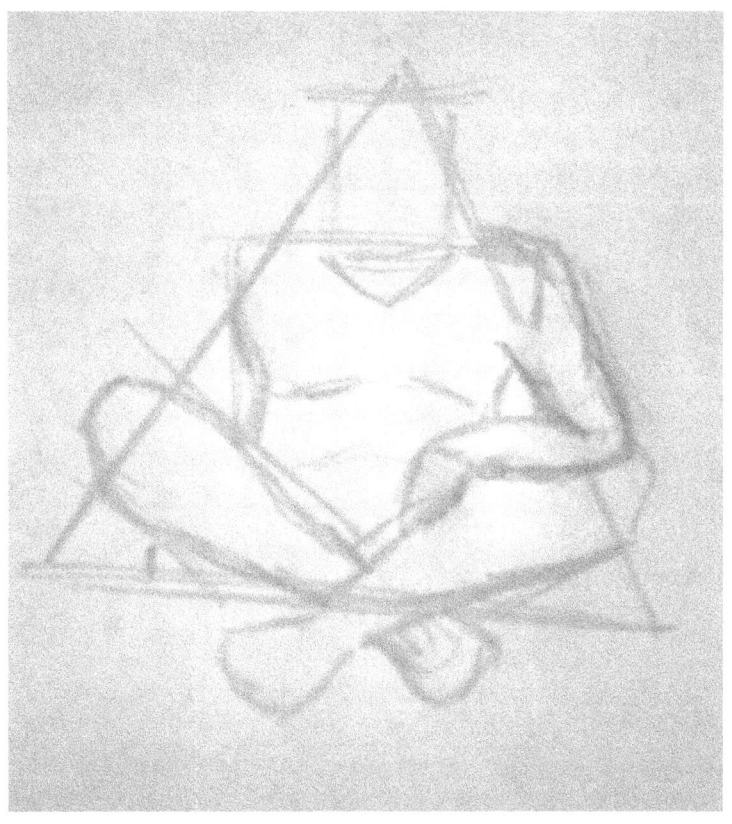

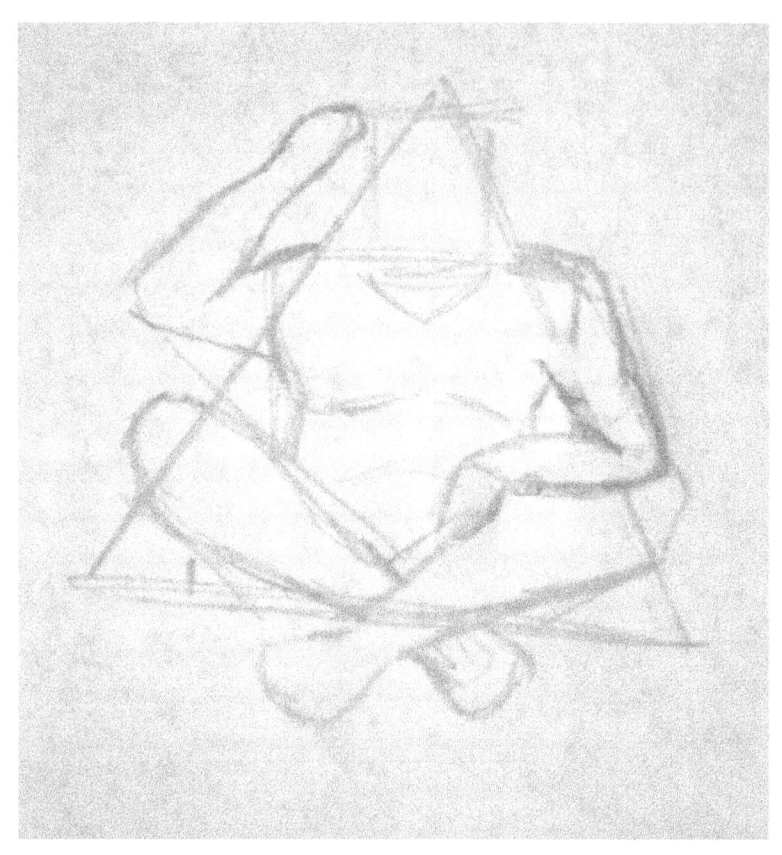

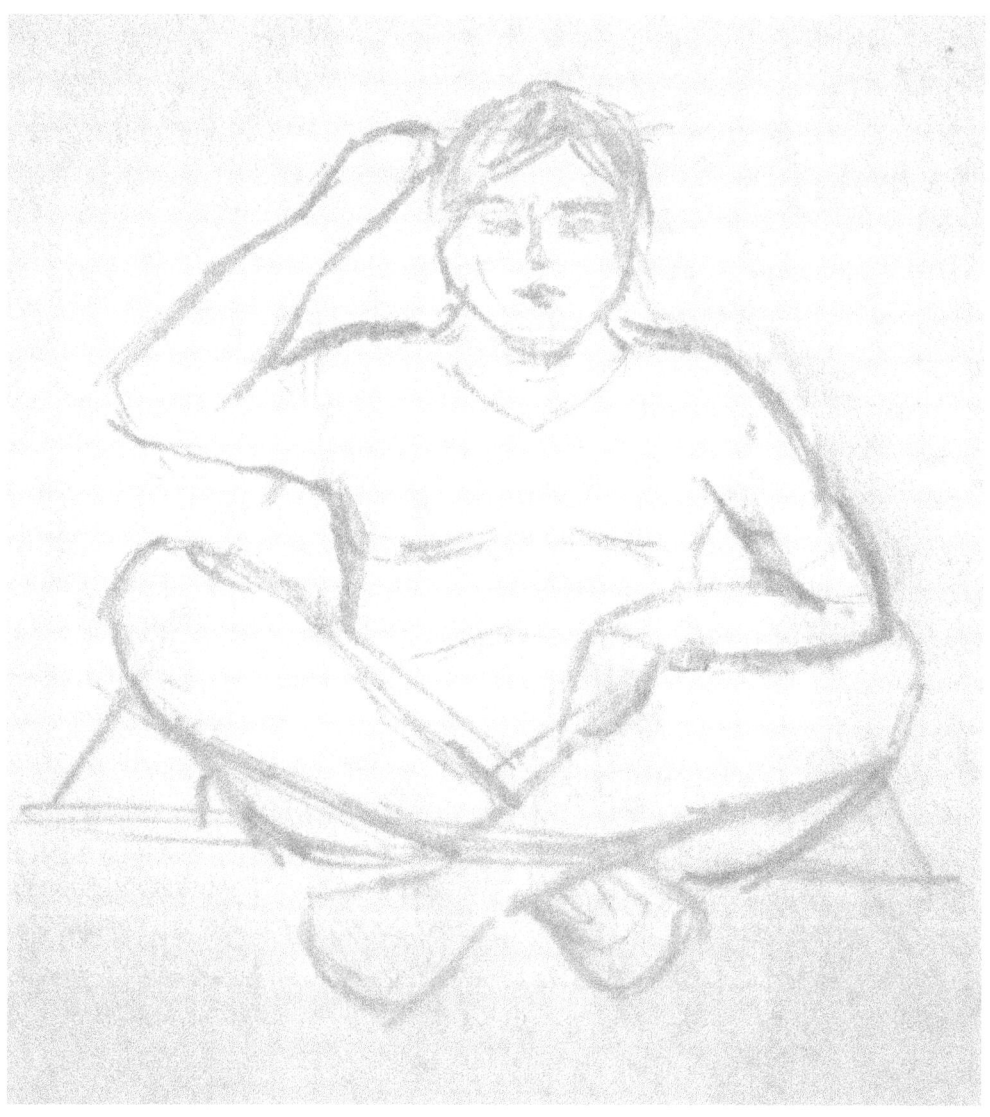

Now, let`s see what other sorts of figures you can draw working within the blocking-in method.

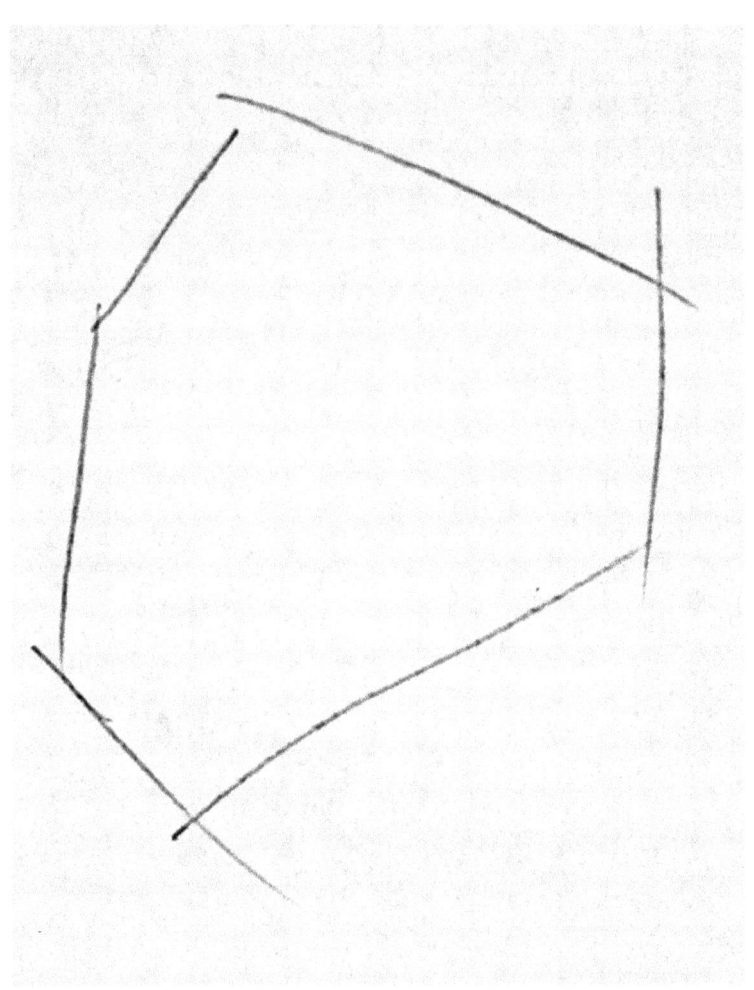

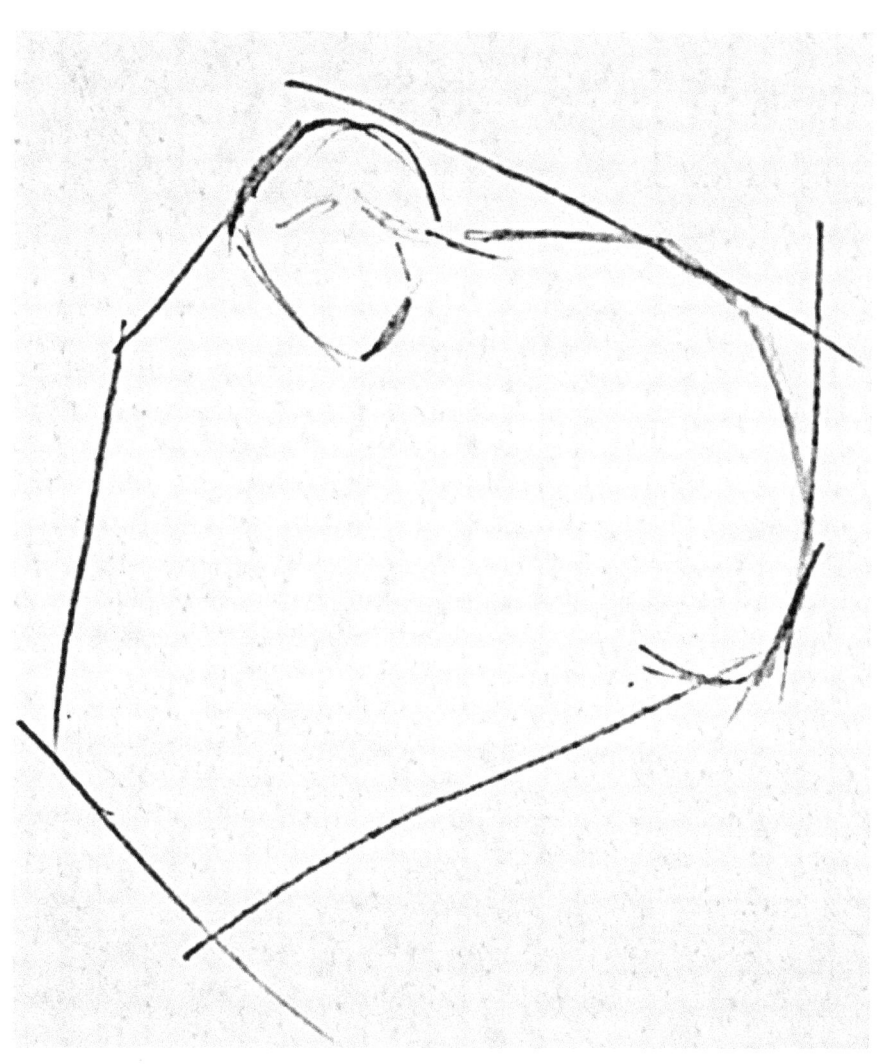

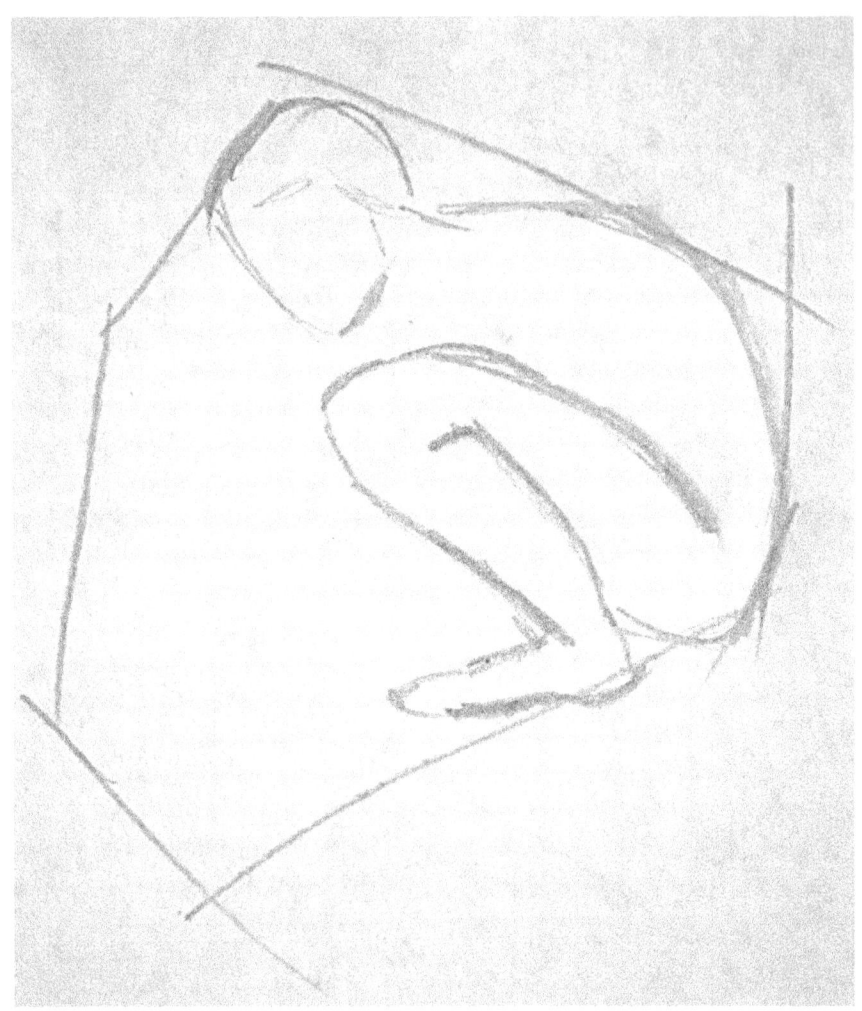

With simple steps you draw the sitting fugure.

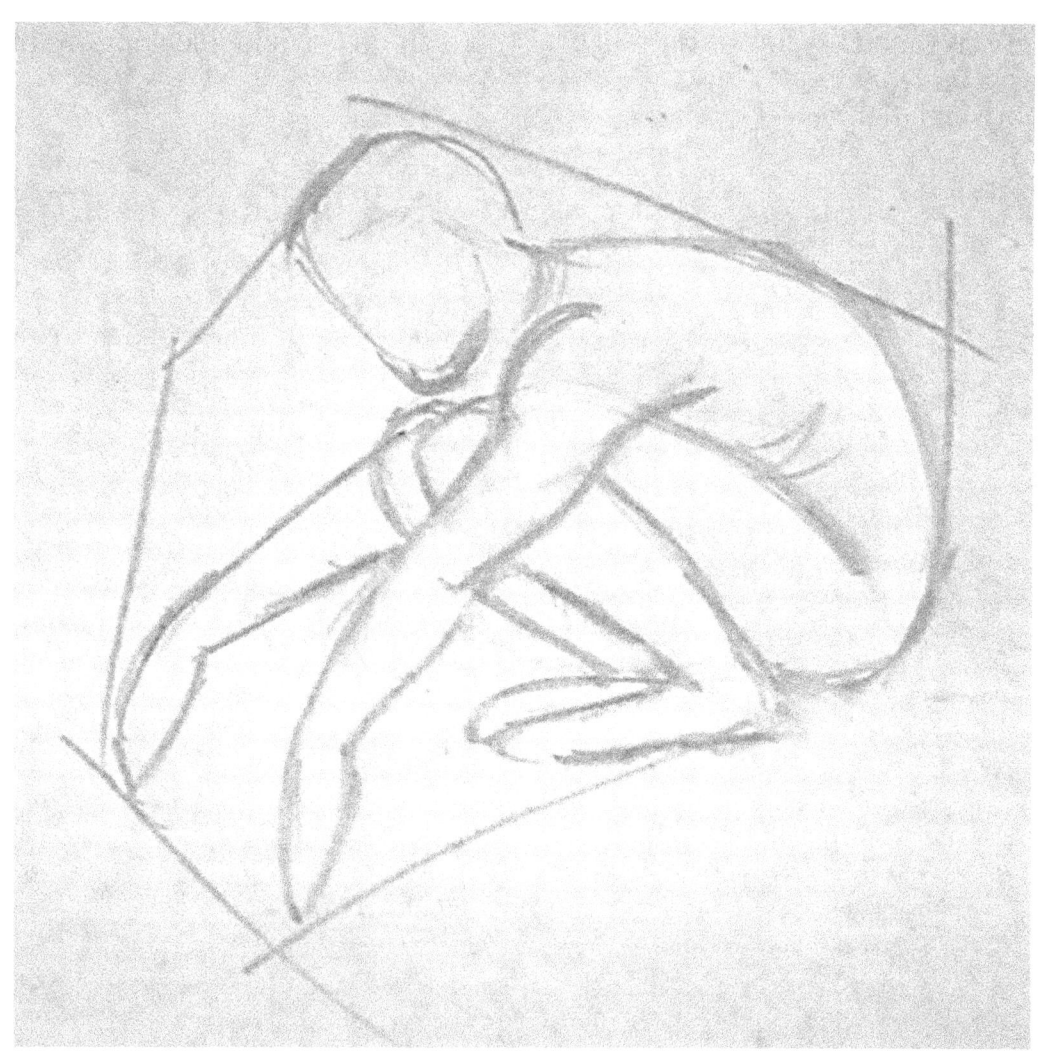

Here is another interesting figure you can get while blocking-in the sportsman figure.

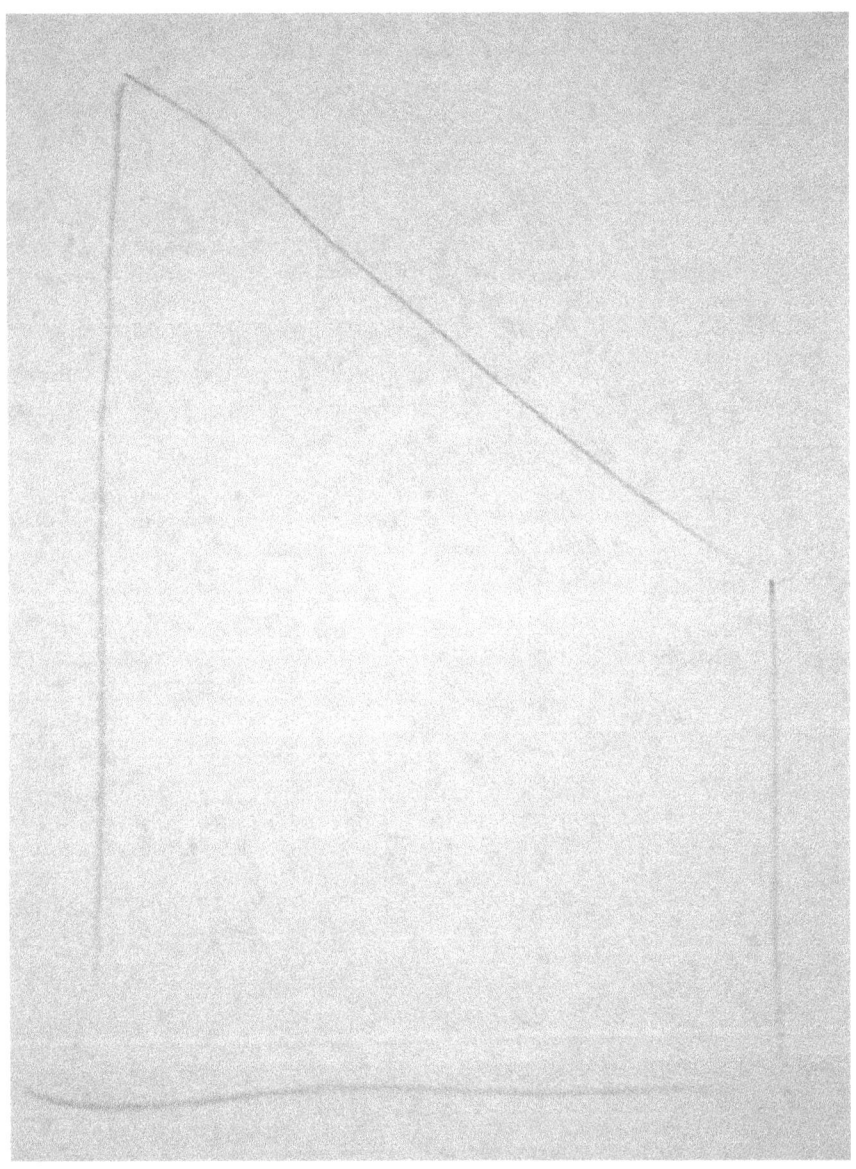

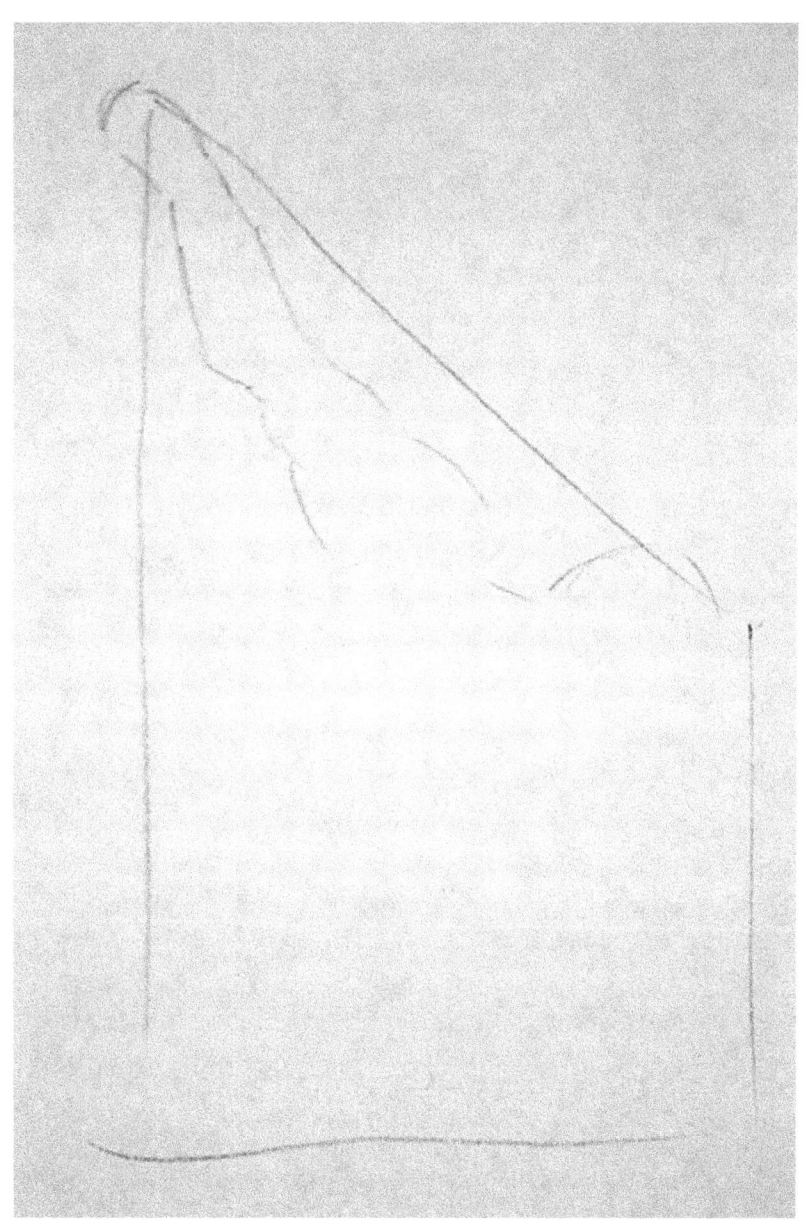

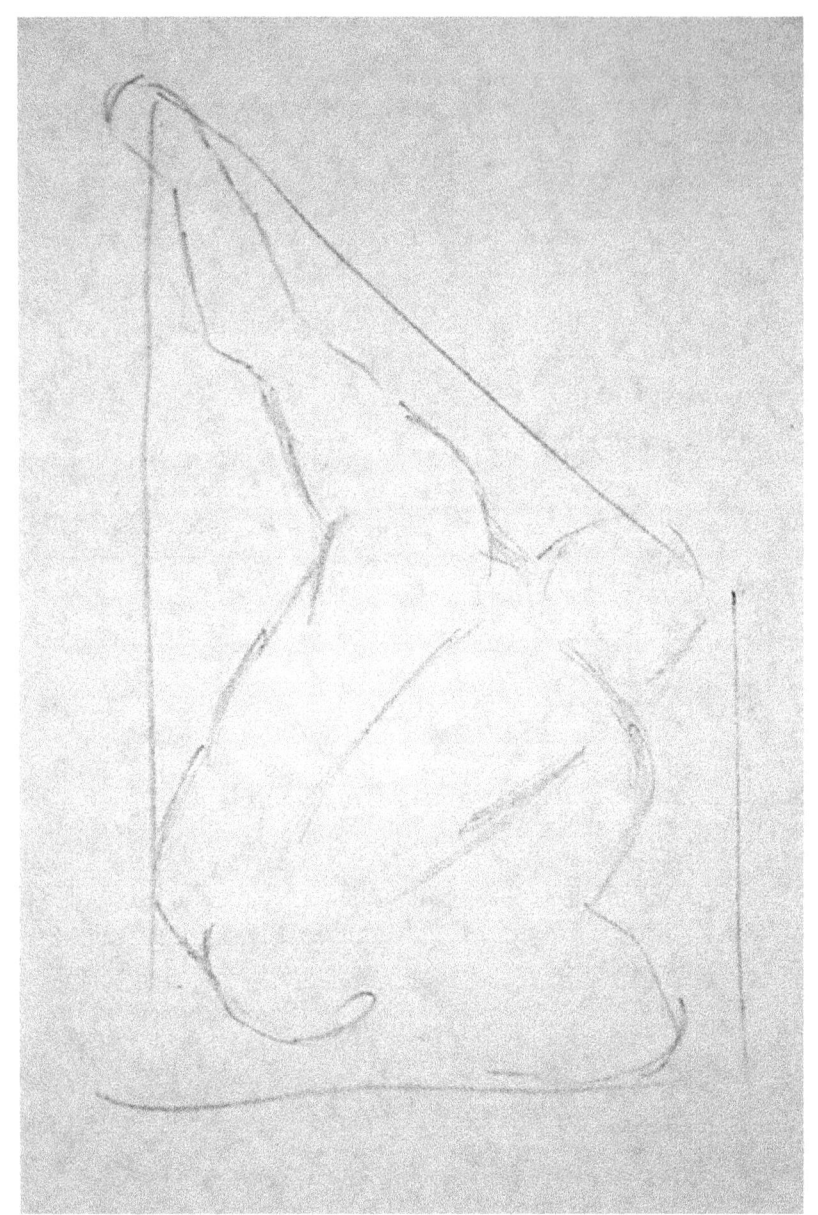

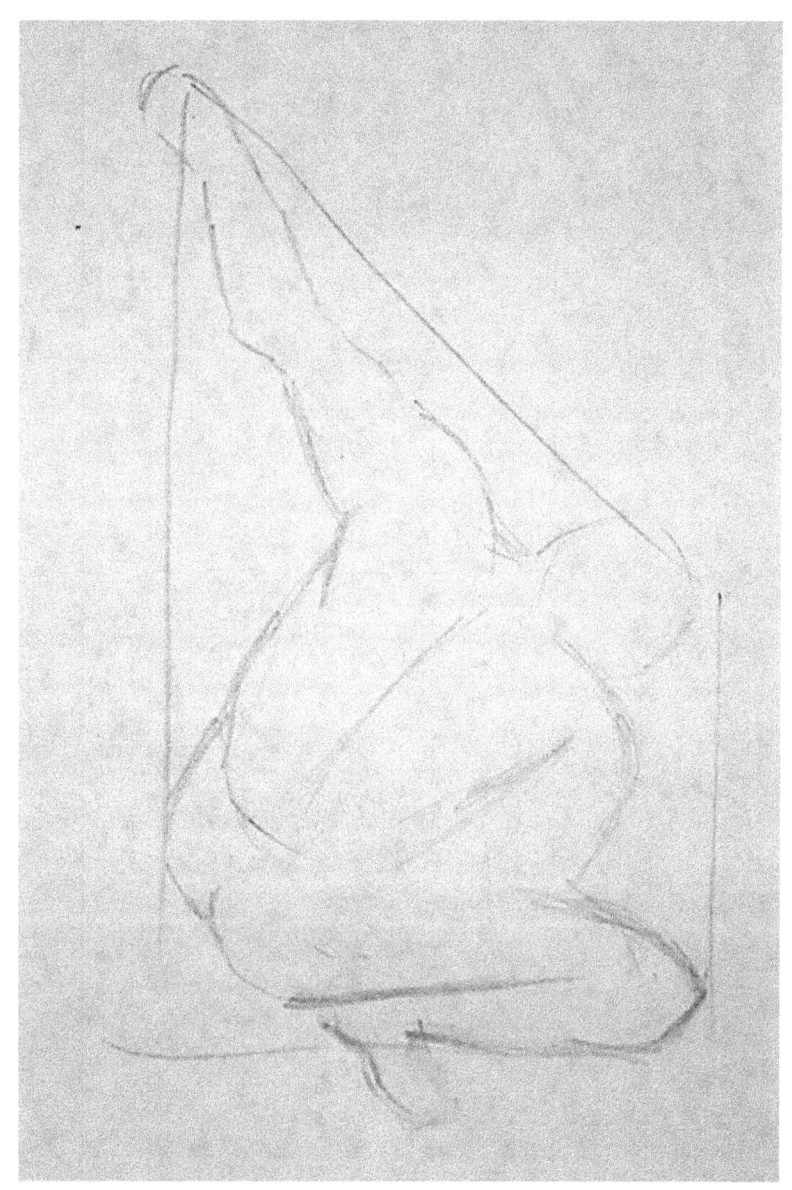

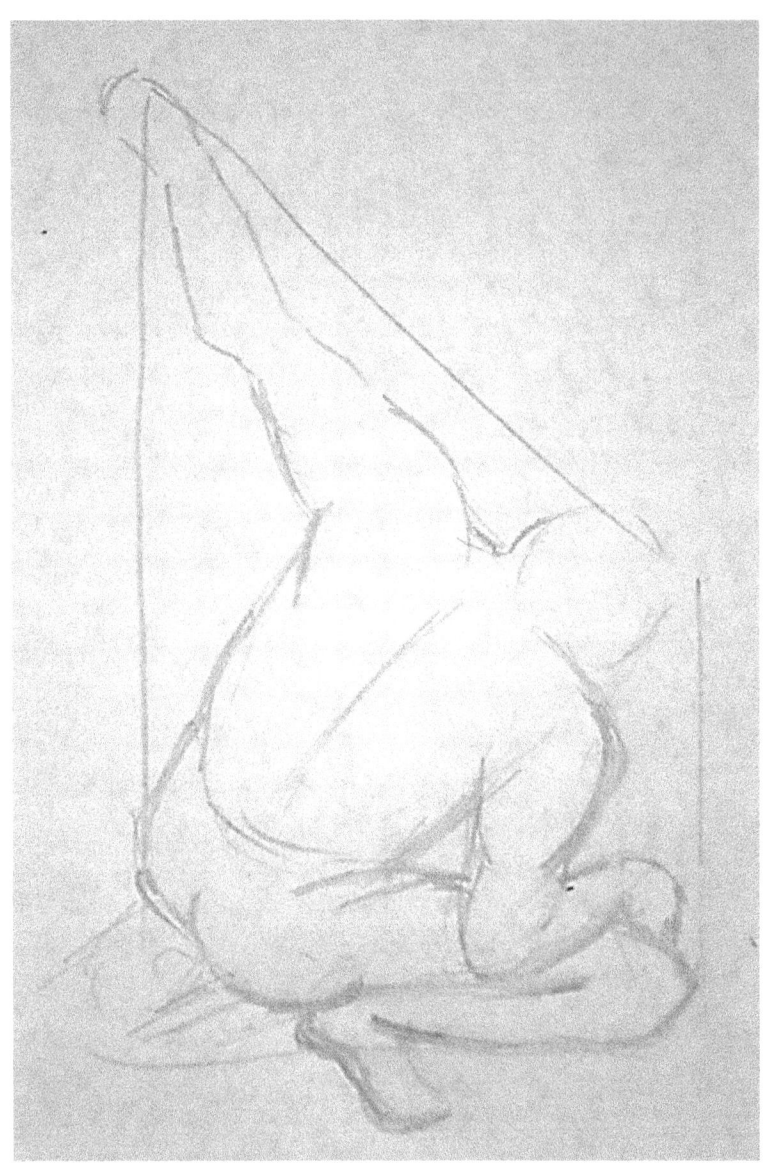

Beautiful woman? Follow the steps below and you will draw it very quick.

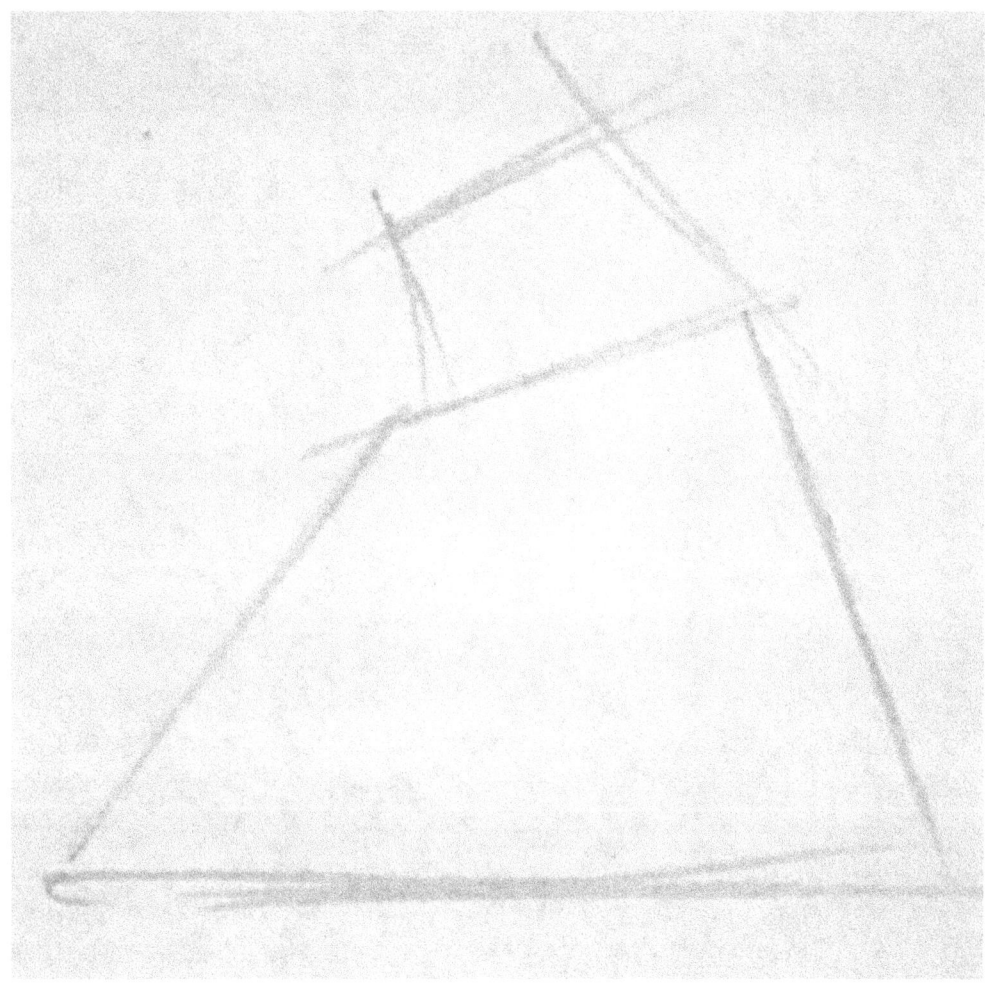

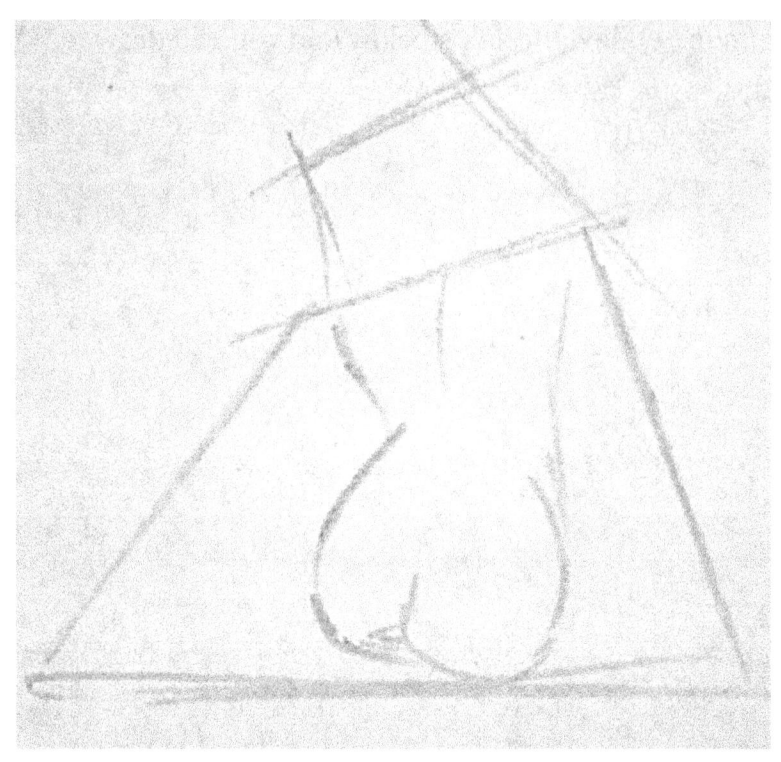

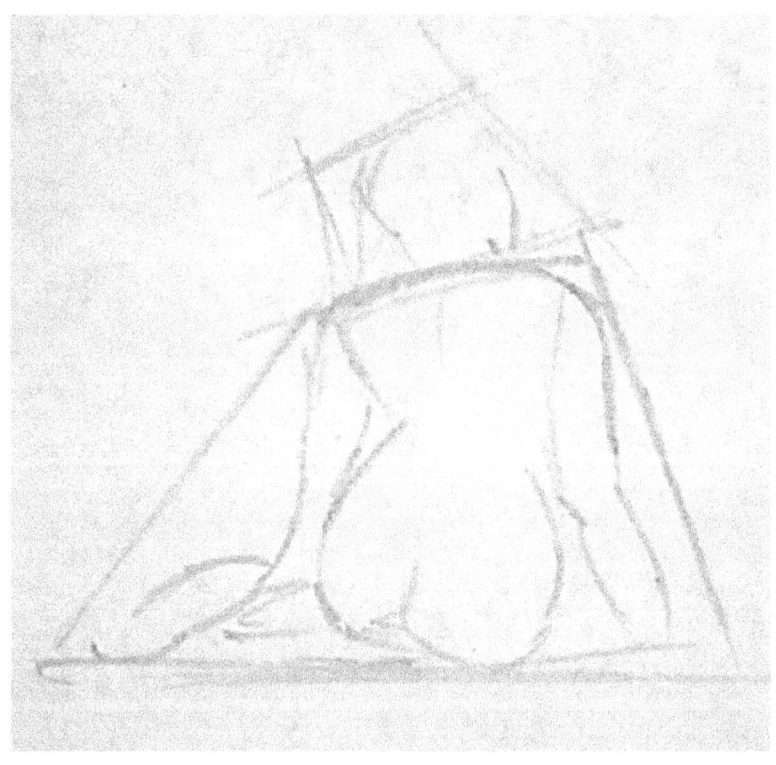

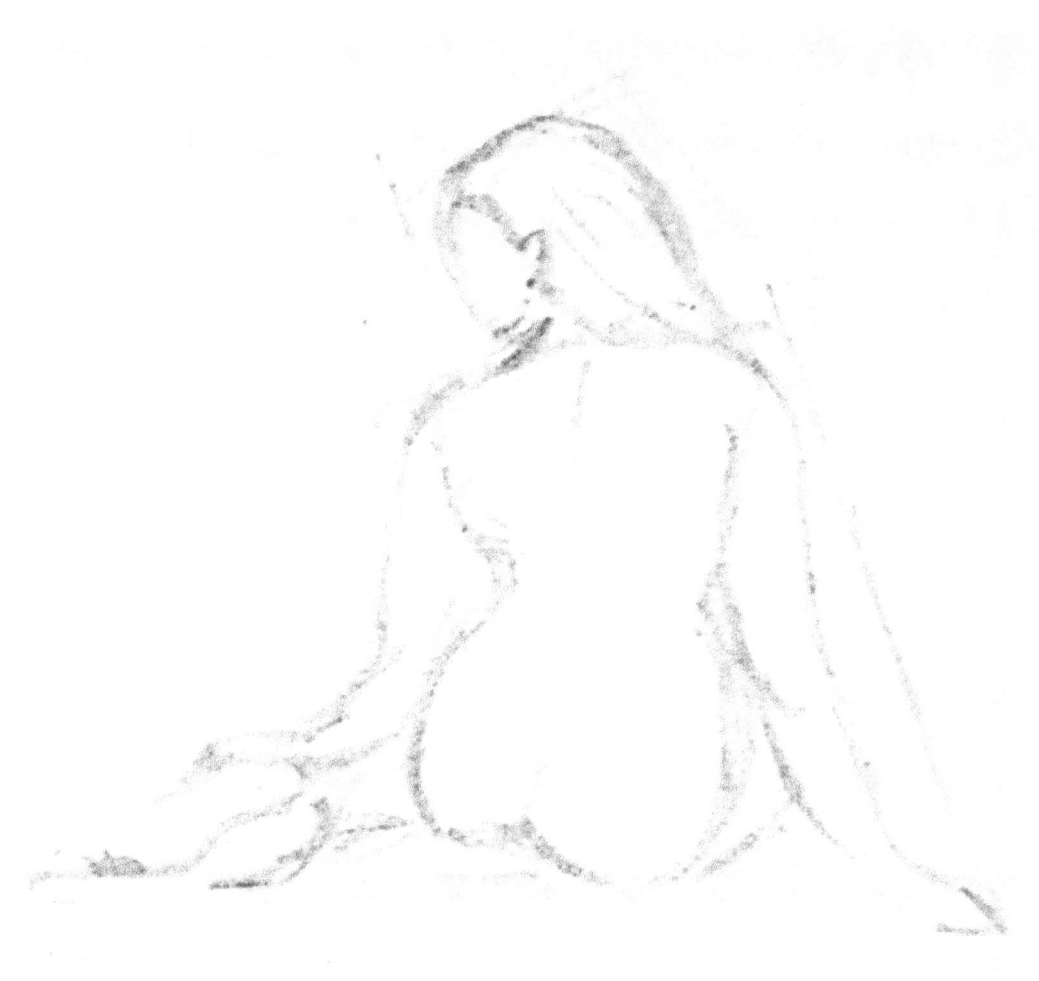

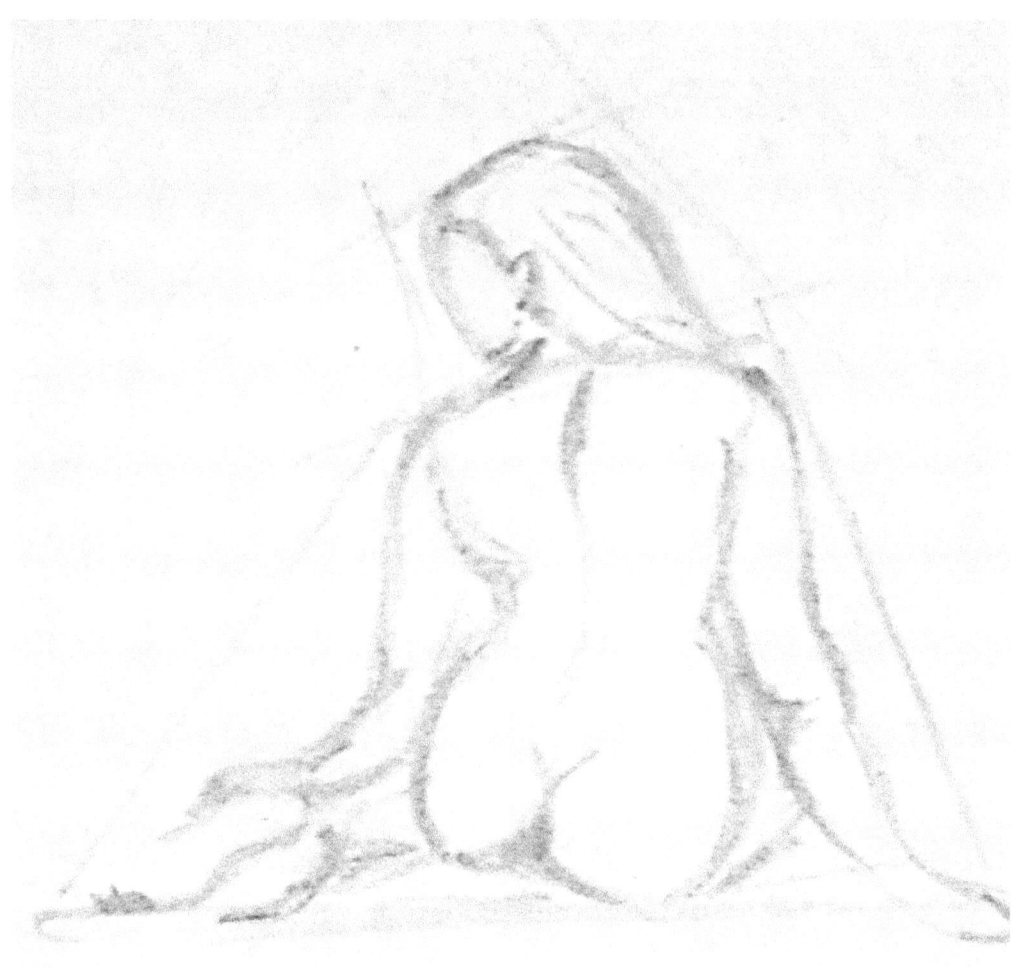

Now you know how to draw blocking-in shapes figures. On this basis you can create something different. Just follow your imagination!

Conclusion

Thank you for downloading this book and I truly hope you found useful information about how to draw the human figure. The next thing for you to do is to buy a block and a pencil and start creating amazing figures of your own.

Drawing the human figure requires a lot of work and practice. The human figure has been a challenge and interest for all artists throughout history. Nowhere will you find a comprehensive book on drawing human figures; the body's proportions, and poses because it is far too extensive an area to cover completely. From that point of view, this book represents only one part of the puzzle called "drawing a human figure".

However, if you find that this book has helped you in some way on your path to becoming a remarkable drawer of human figures, then it has served its purpose.

Appendix

Sites where you can learn to draw human figure

http://www.learn-to-draw.com/figure-drawing/

http://figure-drawings.com/How-to-Draw-Proportions.html

http://coloringpagesjos.net/253458-drawing-body-poses

http://www.quickposes.com/pages/timed

http://pcweenies.com/2013/08/29/the-best-online-pose-sites-to-practice-figure-drawing/

http://www.elfwood.com/tutorial/

http://www.ehow.com/how_6933747_draw-people-using-shapes.html

http://www.dueysdrawings.com/drawing_tutorials.html

http://mydrawingtutorials.com/drawing-body-figures-in-different-poses/

http://www.artgraphica.net/free-art-lessons/drawing-pencil-tutorial.html

http://drawsketch.about.com/

http://www.how-to-draw-cartoons-online.com/

http://www.drawspace.com/

http://www.wysp.ws/practice/course/8444030/

http://www.instructables.com/id/How-To-Draw-8/

www.dragonart.com

http://www.drawingcoach.com/how-to-draw-people.html

http://www.jdhillberry.com/how_to_draw_pg2.htm

http://www.parkablogs.com/content/book-review-strength-training-anatomy

http://alexhays.com/loomis/

Thank you!

Thank you for choosing our book, we hope you found it interesting and helpful.

If you liked the book, please give us a favor to write your review.

We would really appreciate this!

If you would like to have a bonus – **FREE BOOK**, please send the screenshot of your review to this e-mail:

kelly.artbooks@gmail.com and we will send you a **FREE BOOK** in PDF as a **GIFT!****

Hope to see you in our future books and good luck in your drawing experience!

**** in the e-mail subject please mention the name of the book you reviewed and the author.**